IN PRAISE OF MORTALITY

IN PRAISE OF
MORTALITY

SELECTIONS FROM
RAINER MARIA RILKE'S
DUINO ELEGIES AND
SONNETS TO ORPHEUS

Translated and edited by
Anita Barrows and Joanna Macy

RIVERHEAD BOOKS
a member of Penguin Group (USA) Inc.
New York 2005

RIVERHEAD BOOKS
Published by the Penguin Group
Penguin Group (USA) Inc., 375 Hudson Street, New York, New York 10014, USA •
Penguin Group (Canada), 10 Alcorn Avenue, Toronto, Ontario M4V 3B2, Canada (a division
of Pearson Penguin Canada Inc.) • Penguin Books Ltd, 80 Strand, London WC2R 0RL,
England • Penguin Ireland, 25 St Stephen's Green, Dublin 2, Ireland (a division of Penguin
Books Ltd) • Penguin Group (Australia), 250 Camberwell Road, Camberwell, Victoria 3124,
Australia (a division of Pearson Australia Group Pty Ltd) • Penguin Books India Pvt Ltd,
11 Community Centre, Panchsheel Park, New Delhi – 110 017, India • Penguin Group (NZ),
cnr Airborne and Rosedale Roads, Albany, Auckland 1310, New Zealand (a division of Pearson
New Zealand Ltd) • Penguin Books (South Africa) (Pty) Ltd, 24 Sturdee Avenue, Rosebank,
Johannesburg 2196, South Africa • Penguin Books Ltd, Registered Offices:
80 Strand, London WC2R 0RL, England

Library of Congress Cataloging-in-Publication Data

Rilke, Rainer Maria, 1875–1926.
[Duineser Elegien. English & German. Selections]
In praise of mortality : selections from Rainer Maria Rilke's Duino Elegies and
Sonnets to Orpheus / translated and edited by Anita Barrows and Joanna Macy.
p.   cm.
English and German.
ISBN 1-57322-303-4
I. Barrows, Anita.   II. Macy, Joanna, date.   III. Rilke, Rainer Maria, 1875–1926. Sonette an Orpheus.
English & German. Selections.   IV. Title.
PT2635.I65D843213   2005   2004051279
831'.912—dc22

Printed in the United States of America
1 3 5 7 9 10 8 6 4 2

This book is printed on acid-free paper. ∞

Book design by Marysarah Quinn

CONTENTS

ACKNOWLEDGMENTS

We express our gratitude to Clara Westhoff for giving her husband Rainer the freedom he needed while maintaining a lifelong friendship with him. Our thanks also go to Lou Andreas-Salomé for recognizing and igniting Rilke's passion for life. We are grateful to Princess Marie von Thurn und Taxis for providing the poet Duino Castle when he needed it and contributing financial support for his chosen lifestyle. We are indebted to Ruth Rilke Sieber for forgiving her father for not attending her wedding so that he could write these poems. We particularly acknowledge Baladine (called Merline) Klossowska, who, after helping the poet move into the Château de Muzot, generously left him alone to write and pinned above his desk the picture postcard of Orpheus. And we most sincerely thank Nanny Wunderly, who gave Rilke the two standing desks and who was the only person Rilke wanted with him when he died.

To all lovers of life

The great sea
Has sent me adrift.
It moves me as the weed in a great river,
Earth and the great weather move me,
Have carried me away,
And move my inward parts with joy.

—INUIT WOMAN SHAMAN
(quoted by Knud Rasmussen,
cited by Robert Bly in *News of the Universe*)

IN PRAISE OF MORTALITY

INTRODUCTION

FOR A DECADE that encompassed the First World War, Rainer Maria Rilke, already recognized as a major poet, wondered in torment whether he had lost the voice and inspiration that gave rise to his work. Barred from travel during the hostilities, Rilke was cut off from friendships and literary connections that he had cultivated throughout Europe. And he was appalled by the brutality and apparent senselessness of the conflict.

Drafted into the army and subjected to basic training, Rilke served at the Imperial War Archive in Vienna. He was released at the end of six months through the efforts of friends in publishing. Driven by a need to understand the war, he proceeded to Berlin. There, in various ministries, he questioned many key political figures. What he discovered deepened his sorrow and disgust: "People take on the whole a curious view here: knowing that politics by its nature can't always be honest, they immediately come to the harsh conclusion that dishonesty is the best policy. . . . Berlin does not give the impression that anyone is ready or willing to change." To his former wife, Clara Westhoff, he wrote: "Victories, however great, lead nowhere, for there is no inner will for the great changes that would be needed to save the world."

Almost twenty years earlier, in writing *The Book of Hours*, Rilke affirmed the dark side of human experience, and he never flinched from doing so over the five years it took to complete that body of work. Seeing shadow and chaos as the unavoidable ground of all creativity, he would have us not avert our gaze from suffering:

You, darkness, of whom I am born—

I love you more than the flame
that limits the world
to the circle it illumines . . . [I, 11]

Now, in the slaughterhouse that Europe had become, the darkness Rilke allowed himself to see almost paralyzed him with revulsion and helplessness. "If this is true," he wrote his friend Harry Kessler, just returned from the front, "then every line I've written is flawed and false." To an admirer of *The Book of Hours*, Rilke commented, "I'm not living my own life. . . . I feel refuted, abandoned, and above all threatened by a world ready to dissolve entire in such senseless disorder."

In *The Book of Hours*, Rilke had asserted that the poet's essential vocation was to praise, to name in gratitude the things of this world:

I feel it now: there's a power in me
to grasp and give shape to my world. [I, 1]

I will sing you as no one ever has,

streaming through widening channels
into the open sea. *[I, 12]*

But how to praise in a time of such rampant horror?

Not long after we finished our translation of *The Book of Hours*, we found ourselves asking the same question. Like Rilke during the First World War, we at the beginning of the twenty-first century have felt refuted and weighted with dread as our nation mounts preemptive war and arms itself for domination of the world. As our country is assaulted by official lies, the words that once came easily to us as writers dry up now or mock us.

For Rilke, this incapacity was all the harder to bear because only a few years before the start of the war, in 1912, he believed he had broken through to writing the greatest poetry of his life. When the First Duino Elegy came to him, he was convinced that he had begun a sequence that would be his masterpiece. At Duino Castle on the Adriatic, while sojourning alone as a guest of Princess Marie von Thurn und Taxis, he composed the first two Elegies and fragments of others, and conceived the entire work as a series of ten long poems. Yet the years that followed brought frustration. Except for two more Elegies and random passages of others, inspiration deserted him. In 1917 he wrote to Sophie Liebknecht, wife of the jailed Marxist leader Karl Liebknecht: "Perhaps my indescribable suffering at being unable to produce is my most accurate response to the present situation, and I would sooner submit to that suffering than make any concession in the essential."

3

When the war ended, Rilke, at last free to travel, accepted invitations to speak in Switzerland. There a network of affluent friends soon took form, welcoming him as an honored guest and supporting his creative work for the rest of his life. Switzerland, relatively untouched by the war, was a haven that soothed and freed his spirit. After stays at several luxurious homes, he sought a place for himself in the valley of the upper Rhone. Here he heard only French spoken, and German became an inner language, reserved for his writing. The Valais, with its old stone towns and generous vineyards, reminded him of what he had loved in Provence and in Spain. "As I experience it," he wrote a friend that first year, "the Valais is not only among the loveliest of landscapes I have ever seen, but also, to an amazing extent, it offers manifold reflections of our inner world."

If you walk for an hour from the town of Sierre, taking a hillside road between vineyards, you come to the thirteenth-century Château de Muzot, actually a modest two-story stone house. In spite of its simple condition—without electricity or running water—Rilke moved there in the summer of 1921. A Swiss friend handled the finances, another hired a housemaid and ordered a standing desk, while the poet's lover at the time, Baladine Klossowska, known also as Merline, helped him settle in before she obligingly withdrew. She left a postcard pinned above his desk. It was a depiction of Orpheus under a tree with his lyre, singing to the animals. Perhaps Merline wished to remind the poet of their moments together spent reading Ovid's *Metamorphoses.*

For months, the only writing to issue from Rilke's pen was his usual prolific correspondence, in which delight with Muzot and doubts about the wisdom of his choice seemed equally mixed. Then, on February 2, 1922, ten years almost to the week since the first Duino Elegies had come to him, a tide of poetry surged in, unanticipated and unimagined. The lines that took shape, however, did not belong to the Elegies in concept or form. They were sonnets in the classical mode, to honor the mythic singer of ancient Greece who dared the Underworld.

Within three days the poet completed twenty-five sonnets.

And just then, another standing desk was delivered to Muzot. Rilke's friend and patron Nanny Wunderly, doubting whether the first one she sent had arrived, had ordered another. It was at that new desk in the next day and a half that Rilke wrote the Seventh and Eighth Duino Elegies. By the morning of February 9, another sonnet had appeared; and that afternoon, as he walked back from the post office in Sierre, the remainder of the Ninth Elegy and all of the Tenth spoke themselves in his mind. Before the end of February, the ten Duino Elegies were completed, as were all fifty-five of the Sonnets to Orpheus.

In a minor way, we as translators also experienced a breakthrough with these Sonnets and Elegies. After *Rilke's Book of Hours* was published, we cast about for more poetry to translate, trying our hand at various French and German works from the Middle Ages on. But given the alarming direction of world events, and particularly the role played by our own country, everything we turned to seemed flat. After considerable hesitation, we set to work on these great poems of Rilke's later life. They were already so famous and had been translated so many times, and thus we had discouraged ourselves from working on them. Yet when we turned to them, in order to discover the full meaning and beauty they could have for us, we found something new in the originals that spoke to our spirits in this hard time. We began with the Eighth Duino Elegy. The work soon took us where we

5

needed to go, offering ways to dignify our pain for the world and deepen our capacity for gratitude.

ALTHOUGH RILKE had been longing for years to complete the Duino Elegies, it was the Sonnets to Orpheus that freed his voice and allowed him to finish the work he had envisioned.

Why Orpheus? He was the legendary poet with the lyre, whose singing drew wild animals close and caused trees to walk. He was the lover who dared the realm of Hades to bring his beloved back from the dead. The son of a Thracian king and the Muse Calliope, Orpheus was half mortal. But Rilke followed popular tradition by consistently referring to him as a god. Orpheus had received his lyre from the hands of Apollo himself and was trained in its use by the Muses. Eurydice, his bride, one day stepped on a serpent and died from its bite. Orpheus, hoping to retrieve her, boldly descended into the world of the dead. There his music so enraptured the heart of Hades that this ruler of the Underworld let Orpheus take Eurydice back with him on the condition that he not turn to look at her. Together, they made the long ascent through the dark, Eurydice following close behind her husband. But when they neared the light, Orpheus stole a forbidden glance at her—and she was lost to him forever.

Because he was a priest of Apollo, Orpheus incurred the wrath of the sun god's archrival, Dionysus, who sent the Maenads after him. These crazed and jealous women were already maddened by Orpheus's indifference to them. They tore him limb from limb. They threw his head into the River Hebrus, and it floated, still singing, down to the sea.

The savage fate that befell the god is graphically evoked by

Rilke in the poem that concludes the first cycle of sonnets. As we translated, we were reminded of the role that dismemberment plays in many spiritual traditions. In varied ways they all suggest that it is essential to the ongoing nature of life. The breaking to pieces of the Egyptian god Osiris was necessary for his resurrection and the fertility of the land, as was also the case for Tammuz in Babylonian culture. To the primordial Hindu mind, the creation of the world originated in the sacrificial self-dismemberment of the first being, the Mahapurusha. Such ritual self-offering holds an important place in Tibetan Buddhism. Step by step in the powerful visualization process called *chod*, the practitioner dismantles herself and presents the fragments for the honor of the Buddhas and the nourishment of all. Ancient stories about the bodhisattvas, the heroes of the Mahayana tradition, recount the same kind of self-mortification. Far from an expression of grim self-denigration, the Jataka tales suggest a joyously fulfilling, even ecstatic, quality to this act of generosity. For many Christians, the Last Supper of Jesus, with the breaking of the bread, embodies a similarly redemptive self-offering, ritually reenacted in the ceremony of the Eucharist: "This is my body, broken for you."

Rilke's sonnet portraying the death of Orpheus (Part One, Sonnet XXVI) is saturated with these nuances. See how—in a manner that might recall the Eucharist—the dismemberment of Orpheus makes him more available to us as we incorporate his essence and meaning into our lives:

O dear lost god, you endless path!
Only because you were broken and scattered
have we become the ears of nature, and her voice.

7

See how each aspect of the murderous assault is transformed by the god in his refusal to allow it to destroy the basic intention of his life:

> *falling prey to the pack of Maenads,*
> *you wove their shrieking into wider harmonies*
> *and brought from that destruction a song to build with.* . . .

> *Hounded by hatred, you were torn to pieces*
> *while your music still rang amidst rocks and lions,*
> *trees and birds. There you are singing still.*

In a poem written by Rilke twenty-one years earlier for the second part of *The Book of Hours,* dismemberment has already taken place. It occurs as a result of living in modern industrial society. It happens to each of us. Redemption comes only when we acknowledge just how fragmented we are:

> *I've been scattered in pieces,*
> *torn by conflict,*
> *mocked by laughter,*
> *washed down in drink.*

> *In alleyways I sweep myself up*
> *out of garbage and broken glass.* . . .

> *It's here in all the pieces of my shame*
> *that now I find myself again.* . . .
> *I yearn to be held*

in the great hands of your heart—
oh let them take me now.
Into them I place these fragments, my life,
and you, God—spend them however you want. *[II, 2]*

IT WAS the Sonnets to Orpheus that unlocked Rilke's genius, but the Duino Elegies followed within days. From then on, the two bodies of work emerged almost simultaneously. They seemed to generate each other. We were tempted to picture Rilke running back and forth between the two standing desks; but of course each poem as it arose from within him must have absorbed him utterly. Because the poet believed that the Elegies would be his crowning achievement and was long obsessed with the desire to complete them, he underestimated the value of the Sonnets. Yet in a letter from that first week of creation, Rilke spoke of the Sonnets and the Elegies as having "the same birth."

Their form, however, was clearly distinct. The Sonnets to Orpheus were composed in the standard fourteen lines with end rhymes, a classic container that condensed and often intensified Rilke's meaning. Each of the Elegies was far longer and more discursive, and like many of Rilke's lengthier poems, they were written in free verse. Yet despite their differences in form, the two series of poems are charged with the same passionate concerns and illumined with similar insights.

In these concerns and insights, they strikingly recall *The Book of Hours.* Indeed, Rilke wrote to his Polish translator that the Elegies are "a further shaping of the inspirations which had been given already in *The Book of Hours.*" He could have made the same assertion about the Sonnets to Orpheus. Rilke considered *The Book of Hours* the true beginning of his poetic career; now themes from that earlier opus become central again, and bestow a sense of wholeness on Rilke's entire accomplishment. No poetry he later wrote issued from the same spiritual depth, even in Rilke's own estimation.

PRAISE

Orpheus summons us to praise

THE PREVAILING IMPULSE in both the Sonnets and the Elegies is one of adoration—a mounting gratitude for the gift of life. Orpheus embodies that to which Rilke summons us: the act of praise. It is not only the Sonnets that call us to cherish the things of this world, but equally so the Elegies, despite that form's conventional relationship to death and loss. In them as in the Sonnets, praise emerges as the truest and most creative use of consciousness.

In *The Book of Hours*, when Rilke sees us on the brink of collective destruction, with only a short time remaining to the cities we have built, he asks for the chance to perform no other act but that of loving this world more deeply:

> *Dear darkening ground,*
> *you've endured so patiently the walls we've built,*
> *perhaps you'll give the cities one more hour . . .*
> *before you become forest again, and water, and widening*
> *   wilderness*
> *in that hour of inconceivable terror*
> *when you take back your name*
> *from all things.*

Just give me a little more time!
I want to love the things
as no one has ever thought to love them,
until they're real and ripe and worthy of you. *[I, 61]*

Years later, despite the war, this same passionate determination seizes the poet. In the Ninth Duino Elegy, he affirms the transformative power of loving what must disappear:

And the things, even as they pass,
understand that we praise them.
Transient, they are trusting us
to save them—us, the most transient of all.
As if they wanted in our invisible hearts
to be transformed
into—oh, endlessly—into us.

And in a Sonnet to Orpheus, Rilke, seeing impermanence as baldly as any Buddhist, goes on to assert that transience not only shapes our lives, but also constitutes our very identity and our capacity to act:

Ah, the knowledge of impermanence
that haunts our days
is their very fragrance.

We in our striving think we should last forever,
but could we be used by the Divine
if we were not ephemeral?
                    [Part Two, Sonnet XXVII]

.   .   .

THE ACCEPTANCE of impermanence deepens our experience
of the natural world. The knowledge of our essential transience
leads us to identify with all embodied things and frees us from
isolating efforts to hold aloof from the physical realm.

Already in *The Book of Hours*, the young poet had articulated
a perspective that today we might understand as similar to that of
Deep Ecology, which, liberated from anthropocentrism, invites
us to experience our kinship and radical interdependence with all
life forms. In these early poems, as Rilke seeks and defines the
sacred, organic images abound: "my God is dark / and like a web:
/ a hundred roots / silently drinking. // This is the ferment I
grow out of" (I, 3); "you drifting mist that brought forth the
morning" (I, 4); "You run like a herd of luminous deer / and I
am dark, I am forest" (I, 45). And Rilke suggests the kind of
strength that can be ours when we realize our being embedded in
nature: "If we surrendered / to earth's intelligence / we could
rise up rooted, like trees" (II, 16).

Some twenty years later, in the Sonnets to Orpheus, Rilke
gives voice to the same conviction of our belonging to the web of
life. He evokes the changes wrought in us when we allow our-
selves to identify with other creatures, or, as he puts it, to "enter
their dreaming":

See the flowers, so faithful to Earth.
We know their fate because we share it. . . .
If you could enter their dreaming and dream with them deeply
you would come back different to a different day,
moving so easily from that common depth.

12

Or maybe just stay there: they would bloom and welcome you,
all those brothers and sisters tossing in the meadows,
and you would be one of them.

[Part Two, Sonnet XIV]

The most immediate sensory evidence of our belonging is the breath. It represents our transient vitality and responsiveness to change, and also demonstrates our participation in the larger body of Earth, whose breathing we share:

Breath, you invisible poem!
Pure, continuous exchange
with all that is, flow and counterflow
where rhythmically I come to be.

[Part Two, Sonnet I]

You who let yourselves feel: enter the breathing
that is more than your own. . . .
Give yourselves to the air, to what you cannot hold.

[Part One, Sonnet IV]

The sense of mutuality in our relationship with nature is conveyed even more explicitly and hauntingly in the Duino Elegies. In the First Elegy, Rilke suggests that our very capacity to let go of attachments has an effect on the world, allowing more spaciousness for other creatures to enjoy:

Fling the nothing you are grasping
out into the spaces we breathe.
Maybe the birds

13

will feel in their flight
how the air has expanded.

By the end of the Ninth Elegy, Rilke is able to envision—for us and for Earth—a reciprocal transformation. To a real extent, we become each other. It is a sort of resurrection, in which our intrinsic belonging to each other is conscious and complete:

> *Earth, isn't this what you want? To arise in us, invisible?*
> *Is it not your dream, to enter us so wholly*
> *there's nothing left outside us to see?*
> *What, if not transformation,*
> *is your deepest purpose? Earth, my love,*
> *I want that too. Believe me,*
> *no more of your springtimes are needed*
> *to win me over—even one flower*
> *is more than enough. Before I was named*
> *I belonged to you. I seek no other law*
> *but yours, and know I can trust*
> *the death you will bring.*

the dreaded

GIVEN RILKE'S intuitive awareness of our oneness with nature and of the ecological roots of consciousness, it is not surprising that he recognized the dangers inherent in what he called "the Machine." To an extent still rare among poets, his understanding of suffering includes the costs exacted by industrial technology. The Machine, as Rilke sees it, assaults us with its clamor and speed, and takes over so much of life that we humans are diminished, robbed of our strength and our dignity. Furthermore,

14

the poet is bold to perceive the extent to which the Machine requires and, in turn, produces massive concentrations of capital, giving unprecedented power to the abstraction we call money. In *The Book of Hours*:

> The kings of the world are old and feeble . . .
> and their pale daughters
> abandon themselves to the brokers of violence.
>
> Their crowns are exchanged for money
> and melted down into machines.
> and there is no health in it.
>
> Does the ore feel trapped
> in coins and gears? In the petty life
> imposed upon it
> does it feel homesick for earth?
>
> If metal could escape
> from coffers and factories,
> and the torn-open mountains
> close around it again,
>
> we would be whole. [II, 24]

Two decades later, Rilke remained acutely conscious of the increasing mechanization of society and its toll on the human spirit:

> Orpheus, do you hear
> the new sound,

droning and roaring?
Many now exult in it.

Though the Machine
insists on our praise,
who can listen
with all this noise?

See, it rolls over everything,
weakening us
and taking our place.

Since its strength is of our making,
why can't it serve
and not possess us?

> *[Part One, Sonnet XVIII]*

The poet sees that we have yielded such power to our tools of production that they take on a life of their own, disconnected from moral judgment:

The Machine endangers all we have made.
We allow it to rule instead of obey. . . .
It thinks it's alive and does everything better.
With equal resolve it creates and destroys.

> *[Part Two, Sonnet X]*

With anguished clarity, Rilke shows how the Machine deprives us of time, imagination, and community:

. . . Lonelier now,
having no one but each other, not knowing each other,
we no longer meander on curving paths, but race straight ahead.

Only in the mills do the once sacred fires still burn,
lifting ever heavier hammers, while we
diminish in strength, like swimmers at sea.

                              [Part One, Sonnet XXIV]

The Machine gives the illusion of control. Flick a switch, turn the
ignition: we are the masters. It makes it harder to see, let alone
accept, that point where we encounter our fundamental helpless-
ness. It hides from us our death, the sheer fact of our mortality.

RILKE HAD no patience with the fear of death as something
horrid and undeserved, and even less with the easy solace of an
afterlife. Instead, he summoned us to accept our mortality, to free
ourselves from compulsions to conquer or transcend it. The very
fact that we are bound to die can be cause for gratitude, for it
delivers us into the immediacy and fullness of life.

Even as a young man of twenty-five, Rilke sought to redeem
the inevitability of death and presented it as a source of strength.
In *The Book of Hours,* he envisioned a future condition for us all:

No yearning for an afterlife, no looking beyond,
no belittling of death.
but only longing for what belongs to us
and serving Earth, lest we remain unused. [II, 25]

Mortality is a gift that reveals the integrity of our lives, discloses their uniqueness and worth. Rilke conveys this in organic metaphor:

For we are only the rind and the leaf.

The great death, that each of us carries inside,
is the fruit.

Everything enfolds it. [III, 7]

Lord, we are more wretched than the animals
who do their deaths once and for all,
for we are never finished with our not dying.

Dying is strange and hard
if it is not our death, but a death
that takes us by storm, when we've ripened none within us.

We stand in your garden year after year.
We are trees for yielding a sweet death.
But fearful, we wither before the harvest. [III, 8]

In the Duino Elegies, Rilke suggests the rewards of mortality by evoking its opposite: the angelic realm. Angels, after all, do not die. He has a romp with this notion in the Second Elegy, with an extravagant and ironic description of their eternal nature:

Fated to be happy from the beginning of time,
creation's spoiled immortal darlings,
summits of the cosmos shining at dawn,

pollen from heavenly blossoms, limbs of light,
hallways, stairs, thrones carved from existence,
shields of ecstasy, shrines for delight—

After mockingly relishing these notions, Rilke goes a step further. He retrieves the projection. What we humbly assigned to a supernatural level of existence we can now reclaim as our own. But by virtue of being ours, the beauty we reclaim is transient. The angels become

. . . suddenly, each one, mirror:
where our own evanescent beauty
is gathered into an enduring countenance.

But we, when we feel, evaporate.
We breathe ourselves out and gone.

The rewards of mortality become yet clearer in the Ninth Elegy. Here the oneness of our lives calls us to be more fully present.

. . . because simply to be here is so much
and because what is here seems to need us,
this vanishing world that concerns us strangely—
us, the most vanishing of all. Once
for each, only once. Once and no more.
And we too: just once. Never again. But
to have lived even this once,
to have been of Earth—that cannot be taken from us.

We have the opportunity, as the angel does not, to see beauty in the ordinary. It is a human gift, which we alone can exercise:

Praise the world to the angel: leave the unsayable aside....
... show him what is ordinary, what has been
shaped from generation to generation, shaped by hand and eye.
Tell him of things. He will stand still in astonishment,
the way you stood by the ropemaker in Rome
or beside the potter on the Nile.

THE SONNETS TO ORPHEUS bear a dedication: *Written as a grave-marker for Wera Ouckama Knoop.* Rilke had recently learned about the death of this young woman of nineteen, who, in Munich before the war, had been a playmate of his daughter's. He barely knew Wera, but he remembered her beauty and her grace as a dancer. Because these poems were imbued with thoughts of transience, he linked them to her. Only four of the fifty-five Sonnets actually allude to Wera, yet she clearly served as a pretext for the poet's reflections on mortality. Although her early death moved his imagination, the breadth of his vision took him far beyond the romantic lamentation common to the poetry of his era. He was helped by Orpheus, the singing god, who confronted and redeemed the realm of death.

Through Orpheus, Rilke shows how the fact of death, however painful, can illumine our lives. It bespeaks our nature, because, in each moment, we are passing. As he says of Orpheus,

... he has no choice but to disappear,
even should he long to stay ...
so is he already gone where we cannot follow.
                    [Part One, Sonnet V]

We are not to forget this, because

Orpheus, the conjuring one,
mixes death into all our seeing,

mixes it with everything.
    [Part One, Sonnet VI]

Orpheus lets us see the preciousness of life:

Only he who lifts his lyre
in the Underworld as well
may come back
to praising, endlessly.
    [Part One, Sonnet IX]

In the singing of it, the very passing of life is rendered sacred:

How can we embrace our sorrows
or learn how to love,
or see what we lose

when we die? Only your song
over the earth
honors our life and makes it holy.
    [Part One, Sonnet XIX]

The way we can live death at the heart of each moment is evoked in the thirteenth sonnet of the second cycle. Here the journey of Orpheus to reclaim his beloved becomes a journey each of us takes to embrace our finitude and, at the same time, to own our essential identity with the source of life.

Be forever dead in Eurydice, and climb back singing.
Climb praising as you return to connection.
Here among the disappearing, in the realm of the transient,
be a ringing glass that shatters as it rings.

Be. And, at the same time, know what it is not to be.
That emptiness inside you allows you to vibrate
in resonance with your world. Use it for once.

                                                 [Part Two, Sonnet XIII]

Rilke invites us to experience what mortality makes possible. It links us with all life and all time. All who have gone before and all who will follow become our companions in the flow of being. Ours is the suffering and ours is the harvest:

We are one generation through thousands of years,
mothers and fathers shaped by children to come,
who, in their turn, will overtake them.

We are endlessly offered into life: all time is ours.
And what any one of us might be worth,
death alone knows—and does not tell.

                                               [Part Two, Sonnet XXIV]

It is poignant to note that four years later, at age fifty-one, Rilke would die of leukemia. The disease weakened him for some time and was consistently misdiagnosed. His dying was agonizing, but characterized by deep acceptance. In instructions he wrote out for Nanny Wunderly, he specified: "I would prefer to be buried in the hilltop churchyard next to the old church at Raron. Its surrounding wall was one of the first spots from which I received the wind and light of this countryside, together with all the promises which it, with and in Muzot, was later to help me fulfill."

What gives the Duino Elegies and the Sonnets to Orpheus their visceral potency is Rilke's determination to cherish life in direct confrontation with what robs us of life. In the face of impermanence and death, it takes courage to love the things of this world and to believe that praising them is our noblest calling. Rilke's is not a conditional courage, dependent on an afterlife. Nor is it a stoic courage, keeping a stiff upper lip when shattered by loss. It is courage born of the ever-unexpected discovery that acceptance of mortality yields an expansion of being. In naming what is doomed to disappear, naming the way it keeps streaming through our hands, we can hear the song that streaming makes. Our view of reality shifts from noun to verb. We become part of the dance.

A NOTE ON THE TRANSLATION

AS THE SUBTITLE makes clear, this is a book of selections. We offer our translation of thirty-five of the fifty-five Sonnets to Orpheus in their entirety, and major portions of four of the ten Duino Elegies, which in terms of the line count is about a third.

The poetry included here is poetry that we treasure, and that speaks most directly, we believe, to the consciousness of our time. To the modern ear, some German poetry of the post-Romantic era seems sentimental and overblown. Such passages in Rilke risk diluting the effect of the whole and distracting today's readers, accustomed as they may be to a more concise poetic diction. Where we have omitted material, as in the four Duino Elegies, readers may find the entire poem in this volume in the original German.

The Duino Elegies were composed in free verse, and we have translated them thus. With the Sonnets, we have preserved the fourteen-line structure, but have chosen to alter the end rhymes because we felt this permitted greater faithfulness to the poet's tone and register. As we pointed out in our translation of *The Book of Hours*, when the original's regular rhyme and meter are retained in contemporary English-language verse, they convey a singsong quality, as well as a kind of certainty, which contradict the searching character of Rilke's work.

Each cultural moment, with its insights and hungers, brings a fresh perspective to a great work of art. That an opus can elicit new treatments is indeed an indication of its dynamic greatness. As the philosopher Richard Tarnas wrote to us in a letter:

"Rilke's poems, or Rumi's for example, are of such multivalent depth and mystery that every gifted translator brings forth something new and essential from the original, revealing new insights and levels of meaning, different facets of the jewel, different windows into the mystery, further blossomings of the original. . . . In a participatory universe, the true poetic translator brings particular qualities of experience and knowledge that provide essential vessels for the mystery's self-unfolding."

In our estimation, the results we have achieved as translators are directly attributable to the method we employ. We feel very fortunate that, because we are two, our process is by necessity dialogical. Each line was talked and heard into existence as we moved back and forth again and again from the German into varying English renditions. Working together, able to test sounds and ideas on each other, we were perhaps bolder in our choices than if either of us had been working alone.

As was the case with *Rilke's Book of Hours,* every aspect of this work of translation has been collaborative. No portion can be attributed to either of us alone. That holds true also for the introduction and the notes. Eleven years of translating together have engendered a highly intuitive and mutually respectful mode of working. Operating in this way, teasing out together the meanings of each line, has brought us to feel the presence of the poet himself in a vital and immediate fashion. Because we have spoken them aloud and enjoy repeating them, the poems continue to resonate inside our heads and inhabit our lives. So grateful do we feel for our collaboration that we often wonder how or why anyone would undertake the work of translation alone.

DUINO
ELEGIES

The First Elegy

If I cried out, who
in the hierarchies of angels
would hear me?

And if one of them should suddenly
take me to his heart,
I would perish in the power of his being.
For beauty is but the beginning of terror.
We can barely endure it
and are awed
when it declines to destroy us.

Every angel is terrifying in that way.
So I hold myself back,
and let my scream for help
be swallowed by sobbing.

Oh, to what, then, can we turn
in our need?
Not to an angel. Not to a person.
Animals, perceptive as they are,
notice that we are not really at home
in this world of ours. Perhaps there is
a particular tree we see every day on the hillside,
or a street we have walked,
or the warped loyalty of a habit
that does not abandon us.

. . .

Oh, and night, the night, when wind
hurls the universe at our faces.
For whom is night not there?
Longed for and softly disappointing,
it envelops each solitary heart.
Is night easier for lovers, who
can hide from their fate in each other?

Do you still not know how little endures?
Fling the nothing you are grasping
out into the spaces we breathe.
Maybe the birds
will feel in their flight
how the air has expanded.

Can you see? Springtimes have needed you.
And there are stars expecting you to notice them.
From out of the past, a wave rises to meet you
the way the strains of a violin
come through an open window
just as you walk by.

As if it were all by design.
But are you the one designing it?
Were you not always distracted by yearning,
as though some lover were about to appear?

Let yourself feel it, that yearning.
It connects you with those

who have sung it through the ages,
sung especially of love unrequited.
Shouldn't this oldest of sufferings
finally bear fruit for us?

Is it not time
to free ourselves from the beloved
even as we, trembling, endure the loving?
As the arrow endures the bowstring's tension
so that, released, it travels farther.

For there is nowhere to remain.

Die erste Elegie

Wer, wenn ich schriee, hörte mich denn aus der Engel
Ordnungen? und gesetzt selbst, es nähme
einer mich plötzlich ans Herz: ich verginge von seinem
stärkeren Dasein. Denn das Schöne ist nichts
als des Schrecklichen Anfang, den wir noch grade ertragen,
und wir bewundern es so, weil es gelassen verschmäht,
uns zu zerstören. Ein jeder Engel ist schrecklich.
Und so verhalt ich mich denn und verschlucke den Lockruf
dunkelen Schluchzens. Ach, wen vermögen
wir denn zu brauchen? Engel nicht, Menschen nicht,
und die findigen Tiere merken es schon,
daß wir nicht sehr verläßlich zu Haus sind
in der gedeuteten Welt. Es bleibt uns vielleicht
irgend ein Baum an dem Abhang, daß wir ihn täglich
wiedersähen; es bleibt uns die Straße von gestern
und das verzogene Treusein einer Gewohnheit,
der es bei uns gefiel, und so blieb sie und ging nicht.
O und die Nacht, die Nacht, wenn der Wind voller Weltraum
uns am Angesicht zehrt—, wem bliebe sie nicht, die ersehnte,
sanft enttäuschende, welche dem einzelnen Herzen
mühsam bevorsteht. Ist sie den Liebenden leichter?
Ach, sie verdecken sich nur miteinander ihr Los.
Weißt du's *noch* nicht? Wirf aus den Armen die Leere
zu den Räumen hinzu, die wir atmen; vielleicht daß die Vögel
die erweiterte Luft fühlen mit innigerm Flug.

Ja, die Frühlinge brauchten dich wohl. Es muteten manche
Sterne dir zu, daß du sie spürtest. Es hob
sich eine Woge heran im Vergangenen, oder
da du vorüberkamst am geöffneten Fenster,
gab eine Geige sich hin. Das alles war Auftrag.
Aber bewältigtest du's? Warst du nicht immer
noch von Erwartung zerstreut, als kündigte alles
eine Geliebte dir an? (Wo willst du sie bergen,
da doch die großen fremden Gedanken bei dir
aus und ein gehn und öfters bleiben bei Nacht.)
Sehnt es dich aber, so singe die Liebenden; lange
noch nicht unsterblich genug ist ihr berühmtes Gefühl.
Jene, du neidest sie fast, Verlassenen, die du
so viel liebender fandst als die Gestillten. Beginn
immer von neuem die nie zu erreichende Preisung;
denk: es erhält sich der Held, selbst der Untergang war ihm
nur ein Vorwand, zu sein: seine letzte Geburt.
Aber die Liebenden nimmt die erschöpfte Natur
in sich zurück, als wären nicht zweimal die Kräfte,
dieses zu leisten. Hast du der Gaspara Stampa
denn genügend gedacht, daß irgend ein Mädchen,
dem der Geliebte entging, am gesteigerten Beispiel
dieser Liebenden fühlt: daß ich würde wie sie?
Sollen nicht endlich uns diese ältesten Schmerzen
fruchtbarer werden? Ist es nicht Zeit, daß wir liebend
uns vom Geliebten befrein und es bebend bestehn:
wie der Pfeil die Sehne besteht, um gesammelt im Absprung
mehr zu sein als er selbst. Denn Bleiben ist nirgends.

.   .   .

Stimmen, Stimmen. Höre, mein Herz, wie sonst nur
Heilige hörten: daß sie der riesige Ruf
aufhob vom Boden; sie aber knieten,
Unmögliche, weiter und achtetens nicht:
So waren sie hörend. Nicht, daß du *Gottes* ertrügest
die Stimme, bei weitem. Aber das Wehende höre,
die ununterbrochene Nachricht, die aus Stille sich bildet.
Es rauscht jetzt von jenen jungen Toten zu dir.
Wo immer du eintratst, redete nicht in Kirchen
zu Rom und Neapel ruhig ihr Schicksal dich an?
Oder es trug eine Inschrift sich erhaben dir auf,
wie neulich die Tafel in Santa Maria Formosa.
Was sie mir wollen? leise soll ich des Unrechts
Anschein abtun, der ihrer Geister
reine Bewegung manchmal ein wenig behindert.

Freilich ist es seltsam, die Erde nicht mehr zu bewohnen,
kaum erlernte Gebräuche nicht mehr zu üben,
Rosen, und andern eigens versprechenden Dingen
nicht die Bedeutung menschlicher Zukunft zu geben;
das, was man war in unendlich ängstlichen Händen,
nicht mehr zu sein, und selbst den eigenen Namen
wegzulassen wie ein zerbrochenes Spielzeug.
Seltsam, die Wünsche nicht weiter zu wünschen. Seltsam,
alles, was sich bezog, so lose im Raume
flattern zu sehen. Und das Totsein ist mühsam
und voller Nachholn, daß man allmählich ein wenig
Ewigkeit spürt.—Aber Lebendige machen
alle den Fehler, daß sie zu stark unterscheiden.

Engel (sagt man) wüßten oft nicht, ob sie unter
Lebenden gehn oder Toten. Die ewige Strömung
reißt durch beide Bereiche alle Alter
immer mit sich und übertönt sie in beiden.

Schließlich brauchen sie uns nicht mehr,
　　　die Früheentrückten,
man entwöhnt sich des Irdischen sanft, wie man den Brüsten
milde der Mutter entwächst. Aber wir, die so große
Geheimnisse brauchen, denen aus Trauer so oft
seliger Fortschritt entspringt—: *könnten* wir sein ohne sie?
Ist die Sage umsonst, daß einst in der Klage um Linos
wagende erste Musik dürre Erstarrung durchdrang;
daß erst im erschrockenen Raum, dem ein beinah
　　　göttlicher Jüngling
plötzlich für immer enttrat, das Leere in jene
Schwingung geriet, die uns jetzt hinreißt und tröstet
　　　und hilft.

The Second Elegy

Any angel is frightening.
Yet, because I know of you,
I invoke you in spite of myself,
you lethal birds of the soul.

Were the archangel, the dangerous one
beyond the stars, to move down now
one step closer to us, we would die
from the fear in our own hearts.

Who are you?

Fated to be happy from the beginning of time,
creation's spoiled immortal darlings,
summits of the cosmos shining at dawn,
pollen from heavenly blossoms, limbs of light,
hallways, stairs, thrones carved from existence,
shields of ecstasy, shrines for delight—
and suddenly, each one, *mirror:*
where our own evanescent beauty
is gathered into an enduring countenance.

But we, when we feel, evaporate.
We breathe ourselves out and gone.
Like the glow of an ember,
the fragrance we give off grows weaker.

One could well say to us,
"You have entered my blood,
this room, this springtime is full of you. . . ."
What use is that when he cannot hold us
and we disappear into him and around him?

And those who are beautiful—
who can keep them as they are?
Unceasingly in their faces
the life in them arises and goes forth.
Like dew from morning grass,
like steam from a plate of food,
what is ours goes out from us.

Where does a smile go, or the upward glance,
the sudden warm movement of the heart?
Yet that is what we are. Does the universe
we dissolve into
taste of us a little?
Do the angels radiate only their own
outflowing essence,
or is there sometimes, by some oversight,
a bit of ours in it as well?
Are we mixed into their features,
even if only as vaguely
as the openness in the faces
of pregnant women?
The angels themselves
don't notice. How could they?

Lovers, if they understood this,
could say wonderful things to each other
in the night. But it seems
our own impermanence is concealed from us.
The trees stand firm, the houses we live in
are still there. We alone
flow past it all, an exchange of air.

Everything conspires to silence us,
partly with shame,
partly with unspeakable hope.

Lovers, you who are for a while
sufficient to each other,
help me understand who we are.
You hold each other. Have you proof?
See, my hands hold each other too.
I put my used-up face in them.
It helps me feel known.
Just from that, can we believe we endure?
You, however, who increase
through each other's delight,
you who ripen in each other's hands
like grapes in a vintage year:
I'm asking you
who we are.

You touch one another so reverently;
as though your caresses

could keep each place they cover
from disappearing. As though, underneath, you could sense
that which will always exist.
So, as you embrace, you promise each other eternity.

And yet, when that first look
struck terror in you,
and you stood at the window, longing,
and you walked together, just once,
through the garden: Lovers,
are you still who you were then?
When you lift the other to your mouth
to drink each other—drink to drink:
ah, how strangely the drinker fades from the act.

Haven't you been moved, in those early Greek carvings,
by the care you see in human gesture?
Weren't love and loss so gently laid upon the shoulders
that people seemed made of different stuff
than in our day?

Think of the hands, how they touch without pressure,
although there is strength in the torso.
These figures seem to know,
"We have come this far.
This is given to us, to touch
each other in this way.
The gods may lean on us more strongly,
but that is their nature."

We may yearn to come to rest
in some small piece of pure humanity,
a strip of orchard between river and rock.
But our own heart is too vast to be contained there.
We can no longer seek it in a place
or even in the image of a god or an angel.

Die zweite Elegie

Jeder Engel ist schrecklich. Und dennoch, weh mir,
ansing ich euch, fast tödliche Vögel der Seele,
wissend um euch. Wohin sind die Tage Tobiae,
da der Strahlendsten einer stand an der einfachen Haustür,
zur Reise ein wenig verkleidet und schon nicht mehr furchtbar;
(Jüngling dem Jüngling, wie er neugierig hinaussah).
Träte der Erzengel jetzt, der gefährliche, hinter den Sternen
eines Schrittes nur nieder und herwärts: hochaufschlagend
erschlüg uns das eigene Herz. Wer seid ihr?

Frühe Geglückte, ihr Verwöhnten der Schöpfung,
Höhenzüge, morgenrötliche Grate
aller Erschaffung,—Pollen der blühenden Gottheit,
Gelenke des Lichtes, Gänge, Treppen, Throne,
Räume aus Wesen, Schilde aus Wonne, Tumulte
stürmisch entzückten Gefühls und plötzlich, einzeln,
Spiegel: die die entströmte eigene Schönheit
wiederschöpfen zurück in das eigene Antlitz.

Denn wir, wo wir fühlen, verflüchtigen; ach wir
atmen uns aus und dahin; von Holzglut zu Holzglut
geben wir schwächern Geruch. Da sagt uns wohl einer:
ja, du gehst mir ins Blut, dieses Zimmer, der Frühling
füllt sich mit dir . . . Was hilfts, er kann uns nicht halten,
wir schwinden in ihm und um ihn. Und jene, die schön sind,
o wer hält sie zurück? Unaufhörlich steht Anschein
auf in ihrem Gesicht und geht fort. Wie Tau von dem Frühgras

hebt sich das Unsre von uns, wie die Hitze von einem
heißen Gericht. O Lächeln, wohin? O Aufschaun:
neue, warme, entgehende Welle des Herzens—;
weh mir: wir *sinds* doch. Schmeckt denn der Weltraum,
in den wir uns lösen, nach uns? Fangen die Engel
wirklich nur Ihriges auf, ihnen Entströmtes,
oder ist manchmal, wie aus Versehen, ein wenig
unseres Wesens dabei? Sind wir in ihre
Züge soviel nur gemischt wie das Vage in die Gesichter
schwangerer Frauen? Sie merken es nicht in dem Wirbel
ihrer Rückkehr zu sich. (Wie sollten sie's merken.)

Liebende könnten, verstünden sie's, in der Nachtluft
wunderlich reden. Denn es scheint, daß uns alles
verheimlicht. Siehe, die Bäume *sind*; die Häuser,
die wir bewohnen, bestehn noch. Wir nur
ziehen allem vorbei wie ein luftiger Austausch.
Und alles ist einig, uns zu verschweigen, halb als
Schande vielleicht und halb als unsägliche Hoffnung.

Liebende, euch, ihr in einander Genügten,
frag ich nach uns. Ihr greift euch. Habt ihr Beweise?
Seht, mir geschiehts, daß meine Hände einander
inne werden oder daß mein gebrauchtes
Gesicht in ihnen sich schont. Das gibt mir ein wenig
Empfindung. Doch wer wagte darum schon zu *sein*?
Ihr aber, die ihr im Entzücken des anderen
zunehmt, bis er euch überwältigt
anfleht: nicht *mehr*—; die ihr unter den Händen
euch reichlicher werdet wie Traubenjahre;

die ihr manchmal vergeht, nur weil der andre
ganz überhand nimmt: euch frag ich nach uns. Ich weiß,
ihr berührt euch so selig, weil die Liebkosung verhält,
weil die Stelle nicht schwindet, die ihr, Zärtliche,
zudeckt; weil ihr darunter das reine
Dauern verspürt. So versprecht ihr euch Ewigkeit fast
von der Umarmung. Und doch, wenn ihr der ersten
Blicke Schrecken besteht und die Sehnsucht am Fenster,
und den ersten gemeinsamen Gang, *ein* Mal durch den Garten:
Liebende, *seid* ihrs dann noch? Wenn ihr einer dem andern
euch an den Mund hebt und ansetzt—: Getränk an Getränk:
o wie entgeht dann der Trinkende seltsam der Handlung.

Erstaunte euch nicht auf attischen Stelen die Vorsicht
menschlicher Geste? war nicht Liebe und Abschied
so leicht auf die Schultern gelegt, als wär es aus anderm
Stoffe gemacht als bei uns? Gedenkt euch der Hände,
wie sie drucklos beruhen, obwohl in den Torsen die Kraft
steht.
Diese Beherrschten wußten damit: so weit sind wirs,
dieses ist unser, uns *so* zu berühren; stärker
stemmen die Götter uns an. Doch dies ist Sache der Götter.

Fänden auch wir ein reines, verhaltenes, schmales
Menschliches, einen unseren Streifen Fruchtlands
zwischen Strom und Gestein. Denn das eigene Herz
übersteigt uns
noch immer wie jene. Und wir können ihm nicht mehr
nachschaun in Bilder, die es besänftigen, noch in
göttliche Körper, in denen es größer sich mäßigt.

The Eighth Elegy
TO RUDOLF KASSNER

With their whole gaze
animals behold the Open.
Only our eyes
are as though reversed
and set like traps around us,
keeping us inside.
That there is something out there
we know only from the creatures' countenance.

We turn even the young child around,
making her look backward
at the forms we create,
not outward into the Open,
which is reflected
in the animals' eyes.

Free from death.
We alone see that.
For the animals
their death is, as it were, completed.
What's ahead is God. And when they move,
they move in timelessness, as fountains do.

Never, not for a single day, do we let
the space before us be so unbounded
that the blooming of one flower is forever.

We are always making it World
and never letting it be nothing: the pure,
the unconstructed, which we breathe
and endlessly *know*, and do not crave.

Sometimes a child loses himself in this stillness
and gets shaken out of it. Or a person dies
and becomes it. For when death draws near,
we see death no more. We stare beyond it
with an animal's wide gaze.
Lovers also look with astonishment
into the Open, when the beloved doesn't block the view.
It surges up, unbidden, in the background.
But neither can get past the other,
so World closes in again.

Ever turned toward what we create, we see in it
only reflections of the Open, darkened by us.
Except when an animal silently looks us through and through.
This is our fate: to stand
in our own way. Forever
in the way.

If the confident animal coming toward us
had a mind like ours,
the change in him would startle us.
But to him his own being is endless,
undefined, and without regard
for his condition: clear,
like his eyes. Where we see future,

he sees all, and himself
in all, made whole for always.

And yet in the warm, watchful animal
there is the weight of a great sadness.
For what at times assaults us
clings to him as well: the sense
that what we yearn for
was once closer and more real
and infinitely tender.
Here all is distance—
there it was breath.
After that first home
the second feels altered and beset by wind. . . .

And we: always and everywhere spectators,
turned not toward the Open
but to the stuff of our lives.
It drowns us. We set it in order.
It falls apart. We order it again
and fall apart ourselves.

Who has turned us around like this?
Whatever we do, we are in the posture
of one who is about to depart.
Like a person lingering
for a moment on the last hill
where he can see his whole valley—
that is how we live, forever
taking our leave.

Die achte Elegie
RUDOLF KASSNER ZUGEEIGNET

Mit allen Augen sieht die Kreatur
das Offene. Nur unsre Augen sind
wie umgekehrt und ganz um sie gestellt
als Fallen, rings um ihren freien Ausgang.
Was draußen *ist,* wir wissens aus des Tiers
Antlitz allein; denn schon das frühe Kind
wenden wir um und zwingens, daß es rückwärts
Gestaltung sehe, nicht das Offne, das
im Tiergesicht so tief ist. Frei von Tod.
Ihn sehen wir allein; das freie Tier
hat seinen Untergang stets hinter sich
und vor sich Gott, und wenn es geht, so gehts
in Ewigkeit, so wie die Brunnen gehen.

    Wir haben nie, nicht einen einzigen Tag,
den reinen Raum vor uns, in den die Blumen
unendlich aufgehn. Immer ist es Welt
und niemals Nirgends ohne Nicht: das Reine,
Unüberwachte, das man atmet und
unendlich *weiß* und nicht begehrt. Als Kind
verliert sich eins im Stilln an dies und wird
gerüttelt. Oder jener stirbt und *ists.*
Denn nah am Tod sieht man den Tod nicht mehr
und starrt *hinaus,* vielleicht mit großem Tierblick.
Liebende, wäre nicht der andre, der
die Sicht verstellt, sind nah daran und staunen . . .
Wie aus Versehn ist ihnen aufgetan

hinter dem andern . . . Aber über ihn
kommt keiner fort, und wieder wird ihm Welt.
Der Schäpfung immer zugewendet, sehn
wir nur auf ihr die Spiegelung des Frein,
von uns verdunkelt. Oder daß ein Tier,
ein stummes, aufschaut, ruhig durch uns durch.
Dieses heißt Schicksal: gegenüber sein
und nichts als das und immer gegenüber.

Wäre Bewußtheit unsrer Art in dem
sicheren Tier, das uns entgegenzieht
in anderer Richtung—, riß es uns herum
mit seinem Wandel. Doch sein Sein ist ihm
unendlich, ungefaßt und ohne Blick
auf seinen Zustand, rein, so wie sein Ausblick.
Und wo wir Zukunft sehn, dort sieht es Alles
und sich in Allem und geheilt für immer.

Und doch ist in dem wachsam warmen Tier
Gewicht und Sorge einer großen Schwermut.
Denn ihm auch haftet immer an, was uns
oft überwältigt,—die Erinnerung,
als sei schon einmal das, wonach man drängt,
näher gewesen, treuer und sein Anschluß
unendlich zärtlich. Hier ist alles Abstand,
und dort wars Atem. Nach der ersten Heimat
ist ihm die zweite zwitterig und windig.
　　O Seligkeit der *kleinen* Kreatur,
die immer *bleibt* im Schooße, der sie austrug;
o Glück der Mücke, die noch *innen* hüpft,

selbst wenn sie Hochzeit hat: denn Schooß ist Alles.
Und sieh die halbe Sicherheit des Vogels,
der beinah beides weiß aus seinem Ursprung,
als wär er eine Seele der Etrusker,
aus einem Toten, den ein Raum empfing,
doch mit der ruhenden Figur als Deckel.
Und wie bestürzt ist eins, das fliegen muß
und stammt aus einem Schooß. Wie vor sich selbst
erschreckt, durchzuckts die Luft, wie wenn ein Sprung
durch eine Tasse geht. So reißt die Spur
der Fledermaus durchs Porzellan des Abends.

Und wir: Zuschauer, immer, überall,
dem allen zugewandt und nie hinaus!
Uns überfüllts. Wir ordnens. Es zerfällt.
Wir ordnens wieder und zerfallen selbst.

Wer hat uns also umgedreht, daß wir,
was wir auch tun, in jener Haltung sind
von einem, welcher fortgeht? Wie er auf
dem letzten Hügel, der ihm ganz sein Tal
noch einmal zeigt, sich wendet, anhält, weilt—,
so leben wir und nehmen immer Abschied.

The Ninth Elegy

Why, if it's possible to come into existence
as laurel, say, a little darker green
than other trees, with ripples edging each
leaf (like the smile of a breeze): why, then,
do we have to be human
and keep running from the fate
we long for?

Oh, not because of such a thing as happiness—
that fleeting gift before the loss begins.
Not from curiosity, or to exercise the heart. . . .
But because simply to be here is so much
and because what is here seems to need us,
this vanishing world that concerns us strangely—
us, the most vanishing of all. Once
for each, only once. Once and no more.
And we too: just once. Never again. But
to have lived even this once,
to have been of Earth—that cannot be taken from us.

And so a hunger drives us.
We want to contain it all in our naked hands,
our brimming senses, our speechless hearts.
We want to become it, or offer it—but to whom?
We would hold it forever—but, after all,
what can we keep? Not the beholding,
so slow to learn. Not anything that has happened here.

Nothing. There are the hurts. And, always, the hardships.
And there's the long knowing of love—all of it
unsayable. Later, amidst the stars, we will see:
these are better unsaid. The mountain wanderer
does not carry back into the valley a handful of earth—
that is unsayable—but a word, simple and clean:
the blue and yellow gentian. Could we be here, then,
in order to say

House

Bridge

Fountain

Gate

Pitcher

Apple tree

Window

Or, at most, Pillar, Tower—
But to say them, in fact—oh, to utter them
as even the things never thought themselves to be.

Is it not the secret stratagem
of our unspeaking Earth
to have lovers express her abundance
as she drives them into each other's arms?
Threshold: what is it like for two lovers
to step over the same ancient threshold
that so many have crossed before them,
and so many will cross again?

Here is the time for telling. Here is its home.
Speak and make known: More and more

the things we could experience
are lost to us, banished by our failure
to imagine them.
Old definitions, which once
set limits to our living,
break apart like dried crusts.

Between hammers pounding,
the heart exists, like the tongue
between the teeth—which still,
however, does the praising.

Praise the world to the angel: leave the unsayable aside.
Your exalted feelings do not move him.
In the universe, where he feels feelings, you are a beginner.
Therefore show him what is ordinary, what has been
shaped from generation to generation, shaped by hand and eye.
Tell him of things. He will stand still in astonishment,
the way you stood by the ropemaker in Rome
or beside the potter on the Nile.
Show him how happy a thing can be, how innocent and ours,
how even a lament takes pure form,
serves as a thing, dies as a thing,
while the violin, blessing it, fades.

And the things, even as they pass,
understand that we praise them.
Transient, they are trusting us
to save them—us, the most transient of all.
As if they wanted in our invisible hearts

to be transformed
into—oh, endlessly—into us.

Earth, isn't this what you want? To arise in us, invisible?
Is it not your dream, to enter us so wholly
there's nothing left outside us to see?
What, if not transformation,
is your deepest purpose? Earth, my love,
I want that too. Believe me,
no more of your springtimes are needed
to win me over—even one flower
is more than enough. Before I was named
I belonged to you. I seek no other law
but yours, and know I can trust
the death you will bring.

See, I live. On what?
Childhood and future are equally present.
Sheer abundance of being
floods my heart.

Tillich

Die neunte Elegie

Warum, wenn es angeht, also die Frist des Daseins
hinzubringen, als Lorbeer, ein wenig dunkler als alles
andere Grün, mit kleinen Wellen an jedem
Blattrand (wie eines Windes Lächeln)—: warum dann
Menschliches müssen—und, Schicksal vermeidend,
sich sehnen nach Schicksal? . . .

        O, *nicht*, weil Glück *ist*,
dieser voreilige Vorteil eines nahen Verlusts.
Nicht aus Neugier, oder zur Übung des Herzens,
das auch im Lorbeer *wäre*. . . .

Aber weil Hiersein viel ist, und weil uns scheinbar
alles das Hiesige braucht, dieses Schwindende, das
seltsam uns angeht. Uns, die Schwindendsten. *Ein* Mal
jedes, nur *ein* Mal. *Ein* Mal und nicht mehr. Und wir auch
ein Mal. Nie wieder. Aber dieses
ein Mal gewesen zu sein, wenn auch nur *ein* Mal:
irdisch gewesen zu sein, scheint nicht widerrufbar.

Und so drängen wir uns und wollen es leisten,
wollens enthalten in unsern einfachen Händen,
im überfüllteren Blick und im sprachlosen Herzen.
Wollen es werden.—Wem es geben? Am liebsten
alles behalten für immer . . . Ach, in den andern Bezug,
wehe, was nimmt man hinüber? Nicht das Anschaun,
das hier

langsam erlernte, und kein hier Ereignetes. Keins.
Also die Schmerzen. Also vor allem das Schwersein,
also der Liebe lange Erfahrung,—also
lauter Unsägliches. Aber später,
unter den Sternen, was solls: *die* sind *besser* unsäglich.
Bringt doch der Wanderer auch vom Hange des Bergrands
nicht eine Hand voll Erde ins Tal, die Allen unsägliche,
    sondern
ein erworbenes Wort, reines, den gelben und blaun
Enzian. Sind wir vielleicht *hier*, um zu sagen: Haus,
Brücke, Brunnen, Tor, Krug, Obstbaum, Fenster,—
höchstens: Säule, Turm . . . aber zu *sagen*, verstehs,
oh zu sagen *so*, wie selber die Dinge niemals
innig meinten zu sein. Ist nicht die heimliche List
dieser verschwiegenen Erde, wenn sie die Liebenden drängt,
daß sich in ihrem Gefühl jedes und jedes entzückst?
Schwelle: was ists für zwei
Liebende, daß sie die eigne ältere Schwelle der Tür
ein wenig verbrauchen, auch sie, nach den vielen vorher
und vor den Künftigen . . . , leicht.

Hier ist des *Säglichen* Zeit, *hier* seine Heimat.
Sprich und bekenn. Mehr als je
fallen die Dinge dahin, die erlebbaren, denn,
was sie verdrängend ersetzt, ist ein Tun ohne Bild.
Tun unter Krusten, die willig zerspringen, sobald
innen das Handeln entwächst und sich anders begrenzt.
Zwischen den Hämmern besteht
unser Herz, wie die Zunge

zwischen den Zähnen, die doch,
dennoch, die preisende bleibt.

Preise dem Engel die Welt, nicht die unsägliche, *ihm*
kannst du nicht großtun mit herrlich Erfühltem; im Weltall,
wo er fühlender fühlt, bist du ein Neuling. Drum zeig
ihm das Einfache, das, von Geschlecht zu Geschlechtern
      gestaltet,
als ein Unsriges lebt, neben der Hand und im Blick.
Sag ihm die Dinge. Er wird staunender stehn; wie du
      standest
bei dem Seiler in Rom, oder beim Töpfer am Nil.
Zeig ihm, wie glücklich ein Ding sein kann, wie schuldlos
      und unser,
wie selbst das klagende Leid rein zur Gestalt sich entschließt,
dient als ein Ding, oder stirbt in ein Ding—, und jenseits
selig der Geige entgeht.—Und diese, von Hingang
lebenden Dinge verstehn, daß du sie rühmst; vergänglich,
traun sie ein Rettendes uns, den Vergänglichsten, zu.
Wollen, wir sollen sie ganz im unsichtbarn Herzen
      verwandeln
in—o unendlich—in uns! Wer wir am Ende auch seien.

Erde, ist es nicht dies, was du willst: *unsichtbar*
in uns erstehn?—Ist es dein Traum nicht,
einmal unsichtbar zu sein?—Erde! unsichtbar!
Was, wenn Verwandlung nicht, ist dein drängender Auftrag?
Erde, du liebe, ich will. Oh glaub, es bedürfte
nicht deiner Frühlinge mehr, mich dir zu gewinnen—, *einer,*

ach, ein einziger ist schon dem Blute zu viel.
Namenlos bin ich zu dir entschlossen, von weit her.
Immer warst du im Recht, und dein heiliger Einfall
ist der vertrauliche Tod.

Siehe, ich lebe. Woraus? Weder Kindheit noch Zukunft
werden weniger . . . Überzähliges Dasein
entspringt mir im Herzen.

SONNETS
TO
ORPHEUS

Erster Teil
I

Da stieg ein Baum. O reine Übersteigung!
O Orpheus singt! O hoher Baum im Ohr!
Und alles schwieg. Doch selbst in der Verschweigung
ging neuer Anfang, Wink und Wandlung vor.

Tiere aus Stille drangen aus dem klaren
gelösten Wald von Lager und Genist;
und da ergab sich, daß sie nicht aus List
und nicht aus Angst in sich so leise waren,

sondern aus Hören. Brüllen, Schrei, Geröhr
schien klein in ihren Herzen. Und wo eben
kaum eine Hütte war, dies zu empfangen,

ein Unterschlupf aus dunkelstem Verlangen
mit einem Zugang, dessen Pfosten beben,—
da schufst du ihnen Tempel im Gehör.

Part One

I

A tree rose there. What pure arising.
Oh, Orpheus sings! Now I can hear the tree.
Then all went silent. But even in the silence
was signal, beginning, change.

Out of the stillness of the unbound forest,
animals came forth from dens and nests.
And it was not fear or cunning
that made them be so quiet,

but the desire to listen. Every cry, howl, roar
was stilled inside them. And where
not even a hut stood

or the scantest shelter
to contain their ineffable longing,
you made them, from their listening, a temple.

Erster Teil
II

Und fast ein Mädchen wars und ging hervor
aus diesem einigen Glück von Sang und Leier
und glänzte klar durch ihre Frühlingsschleier
und machte sich ein Bett in meinem Ohr.

Und schlief in mir. Und alles war ihr Schlaf.
Die Bäume, die ich je bewundert, diese
fühlbare Ferne, die gefühlte Wiese
und jedes Staunen, das mich selbst betraf.

Sie schlief die Welt. Singender Gott, wie hast
du sie vollendet, daß sie nicht begehrte,
erst wach zu sein? Sieh, sie erstand und schlief.

Wo ist ihr Tod? O, wirst du dies Motiv
erfinden noch, eh sich dein Lied verzehrte?—
Wo sinkt sie hin aus mir? . . . Ein Mädchen fast . . .

Part One
II

It was as though a girl came forth
from the marriage of song and lyre,
shining like springtime.
She became inseparable from my own hearing.

She slept in me. Everything was in her sleep:
the trees I had loved, the distances
that had opened, the meadows—
all that had ever moved me.

She slept the world. Singing god, how
have you fashioned her, that she does not long
to have once been awake? See: she took form and slept.

Where is her death? Will you discover
the answer before your song is spent?
If I forget her, will she disappear?

Ein Gott vermags. Wie aber, sag mir, soll
ein Mann ihm folgen durch die schmale Leier?
Sein Sinn ist Zwiespalt. An der Kreuzung zweier
Herzwege steht kein Tempel für Apoll.

Gesang, wie du ihn lehrst, ist nicht Begehr,
nicht Werbung um ein endlich noch Erreichtes;
Gesang ist Dasein. Für den Gott ein Leichtes.
Wann aber *sind* wir? Und wann wendet er

an unser Sein die Erde und die Sterne?
Dies *ists* nicht, Jüngling, daß du liebst, wenn auch
die Stimme dann den Mund dir aufstößt,—lerne

vergessen, daß du aufsangst. Das verrinnt.
In Wahrheit singen, ist ein andrer Hauch.
Ein Hauch um nichts. Ein Wehn im Gott. Ein Wind.

Part One
III

A god can do it. But tell me how
a person can flow like that through the slender lyre.
Our mind is split. At the crossroads in our heart
stands no temple for Apollo.

Song, as you teach us, is not a grasping,
not a seeking for some final consummation.
To sing is to be. Easy for a god.
But when do *we* simply be? When do *we*

become one with earth and stars?
It is not achieved, young friend, by being in love,
however vibrant that makes your voice.

Learn to forget you sang like that. It passes.
Truly to sing takes another kind of breath.
A breath in the void. A shudder in God. A wind.

O ihr zärtlichen, tretet zuweilen
in den Atem, der euch nicht meint,
laßt ihn an eueren Wangen sich teilen,
hinter euch zittert er, wieder vereint.

O ihr Seligen, o ihr Heilen,
die ihr der Anfang der Herzen scheint.
Bogen der Pfeile und Ziele von Pfeilen,
ewiger glänzt euer Lächeln verweint.

Fürchtet euch nicht zu leiden, die Schwere,
gebt sie zurück an der Erde Gewicht;
schwer sind die Berge, schwer sind die Meere.

Selbst die als Kinder ihr pflanztet, die Bäume,
wurden zu schwer längst; ihr trüget sie nicht.
Aber die Lüfte . . . aber die Räume . . .

Part One
IV

You who let yourselves feel: enter the breathing
that is more than your own.
Let it brush your cheeks
as it divides and rejoins behind you.

Blessed ones, whole ones,
you where the heart begins:
You are the bow that shoots the arrows
and you are the target.

Fear not the pain. Let its weight fall back
into the earth;
for heavy are the mountains, heavy the seas.

The trees you planted in childhood have grown
too heavy. You cannot bring them along.
Give yourselves to the air, to what you cannot hold.

Errichtet keinen Denkstein. Laßt die Rose
nur jedes Jahr zu seinen Gunsten blühn.
Denn Orpheus ists. Seine Metamorphose
in dem und dem. Wir sollen uns nicht mühn

um andre Namen. Ein für alle Male
ists Orpheus, wenn es singt. Er kommt und geht.
Ists nicht schon viel, wenn er die Rosenschale
um ein paar Tage manchmal übersteht?

O wie er schwinden muß, daß ihrs begrifft!
Und wenn ihm selbst auch bangte, daß er schwände.
Indem sein Wort das Hiersein übertrifft,

ist er schon dort, wohin ihrs nicht begleitet.
Der Leier Gitter zwangt ihm nicht die Hände.
Und er gehorcht, indem er überschreitet.

Part One
V

Erect no gravestone. Just let the rose
bloom every year for him.
For this is Orpheus: metamorphosis
into one thing, then another.

We need not search for other names.
It is Orpheus in the singing, once and for all time.
He comes and goes. Is it not enough
that sometimes he outlasts a bowl of roses?

Oh, if you could understand—he has no choice
    but to disappear,
even should he long to stay. As his song
exceeds the present moment,

so is he already gone where we cannot follow.
The lyre's strings do not hold back his hands.
It is in moving farther on that he obeys.

Ist er ein Hiesiger? Nein, aus beiden
Reichen erwuchs seine weite Natur.
Kundiger böge die Zweige der Weiden,
wer die Wurzeln der Weiden erfuhr.

Geht ihr zu Bette, so laßt auf dem Tische
Brot nicht und Milch nicht; die Toten ziehts—.
Aber er, der Beschwörende, mische
unter der Milde des Augenlids

ihre Erscheinung in alles Geschaute;
und der Zauber von Erdrauch und Raute
sei ihm so wahr wie der klarste Bezug.

Nichts kann das gültige Bild ihm verschlimmern;
sei es aus Gräbern, sei es aus Zimmern,
rühme er Fingerring, Spange und Krug.

Part One
VI

Is Orpheus of this world? No. The vastness of his nature
is born of both realms.
If you know how the willow is shaped underground,
you can see it more clearly above.

We are told not to leave food
on the table overnight: it draws the dead.
But Orpheus, the conjuring one,
mixes death into all our seeing,

mixes it with everything.
The wafting of smoke and incense
is as real to him as the most solid thing.

Nothing can sully what he beholds.
He praises the ring, the bracelet, the pitcher,
whether it comes from a bedroom or a grave.

Rühmen, das ists! Ein zum Rühmen Bestellter,
ging er hervor wie das Erz aus des Steins
Schweigen. Sein Herz, o vergängliche Kelter
eines den Menschen unendlichen Weins.

Nie versagt ihm die Stimme am Staube,
wenn ihn das göttliche Beispiel ergreift.
Alles wird Weinberg, alles wird Traube,
in seinem fühlenden Süden gereift.

Nicht in den Grüften der Könige Moder
straft ihm die Rühmung Lügen, oder
daß von den Göttern ein Schatten fällt.

Er ist einer der bleibenden Boten,
der noch weit in die Türen der Toten
Schalen mit rühmlichen Früchten hält.

Part One
VII

*[handwritten: It is all about praising –
Created to praise!]*

It is all about praising.
Created to praise, his heart
is a winepress destined to break,
that makes for us an eternal wine.

His voice never chokes with dust
when words for the sacred come through.
All becomes vineyard. All becomes grape,
ripening in the southland of his being.

Nothing, not even the rot
in royal tombs, or the shadow cast by a god,
gives the lie to his praising.

He is ever the messenger,
venturing far through the doors of the dead,
bearing a bowl of fresh-picked fruit.

[handwritten: same as jungs on cratos?]

79

Erster Teil
IX

Nur wer die Leier schon hob
auch unter Schatten,
darf das unendliche Lob
ahnend erstatten.

Nur wer mit Toten vom Mohn
aß, von dem ihren,
wird nicht den leisesten Ton
wieder verlieren.

Mag auch die Spieglung im Teich
oft uns verschwimmen:
Wisse das Bild.

Erst in dem Doppelbereich
werden die Stimmen
ewig und mild.

Part One
IX

Only he who lifts his lyre
in the Underworld as well
may come back
to praising, endlessly.

Only he who has eaten
the food of the dead
will make music so clear
that even the softest tone is heard.

Though the reflection in the pool
often ripples away,
take the image within you.

Only in the double realm
do our voices carry
all they can say.

Sieh den Himmel. Heißt kein Sternbild »Reiter«?
Denn dies ist uns seltsam eingeprägt:
dieser Stolz aus Erde. Und ein Zweiter,
der ihn treibt und hält und den er trägt.

Ist nicht so, gejagt und dann gebändigt,
diese sehnige Natur des Seins?
Weg und Wendung. Doch ein Druck verständigt.
Neue Weite. Und die zwei sind eins.

Aber *sind* sie's? Oder meinen beide
nicht den Weg, den sie zusammen tun?
Namenlos schon trennt sie Tisch und Weide.

Auch die sternische Verbindung trügt.
Doch uns freue eine Weile nun
der Figur zu glauben. Das genügt.

Part One
XI

Look at the sky. Is there no constellation called Rider?
For the image is imprinted on the mind:
this arrogance made from Earth and a second one astride,
driving him and holding him back.

Hunted, then harnessed: isn't this
the sinewy nature of our being?
Path and turning, a touch to guide.
New distances. And the two are one.

But are they? Or is it only the going
that unites them? When they stop
they belong again to table or pasture.

The starry patterns fool us, too. Still,
it pleases us for a moment
to believe in them. That is all we need.

Heil dem Geist, der uns verbinden mag;
denn wir leben wahrhaft in Figuren.
Und mit kleinen Schritten gehn die Uhren
neben unserm eigentlichen Tag.

Ohne unsern wahren Platz zu kennen,
handeln wir aus wirklichem Bezug.
Die Antennen fühlen die Antennen,
und die leere Ferne trug . . .

Reine Spannung. O Musik der Kräfte!
Ist nicht durch die läßlichen Geschäfte
jede Störung von dir abgelenkt?

Selbst wenn sich der Bauer sorgt und handelt,
wo die Saat in Sommer sich verwandelt,
reicht er niemals hin. Die Erde *schenkt*.

Bless the spirit that makes connections,
for truly we live in what we imagine.
Clocks move alongside our real life
with steps that are ever the same.

Though we do not know our exact location,
we are held in place by what links us.
Across trackless distances
antennas sense each other.

Pure attention, the essence of the powers!
Distracted by each day's doing,
how can we hear the signals?

Even as the farmer labors
there where the seed turns into summer,
it is not his work. It is Earth who gives.

Erster Teil
XIII

Voller Apfel, Birne und Banane,
Stachelbeere . . . Alles dieses spricht
Tod und Leben in den Mund . . . Ich ahne . . .
Lest es einem Kind vom Angesicht,

wenn es sie erschmeckt. Dies kommt von weit.
Wird euch langsam namenlos im Munde?
Wo sonst Worte waren, fließen Funde,
aus dem Fruchtfleisch überrascht befreit.

Wagt zu sagen, was ihr Apfel nennt.
Diese Süße, die sich erst verdichtet,
um, im Schmecken leise aufgerichtet,

klar zu werden, wach und transparent,
doppeldeutig, sonnig, erdig, hiesig—:
O Erfahrung, Fühlung, Freude—, riesig!

Part One
XIII

Full round apple, peach, pear, blackberry.
Each speaks life and death
into the mouth. Look
at the face of a child eating them.

The tastes come from afar
and slowly grow nameless on the tongue.
Where there were words, discoveries flow,
released from within the fruit.

What we call apple—dare to say what it is,
this sweetness which first condensed itself
so that, in the tasting, it may burst forth

and be known in all its meanings
of sun and earth and here.
How immense, the act and the pleasure of it.

Zu unterst der Alte, verworrn,
all der Erbauten
Wurzel, verborgener Born,
den sie nie schauten.

Sturmhelm und Jägerhorn,
Spruch von Ergrauten,
Männer im Bruderzorn,
Frauen wie Lauten . . .

Drängender Zweig an Zweig,
nirgends ein freier . . .
Einer! o steig . . . o steig . . .

Aber sie brechen noch.
Dieser erst oben doch
biegt sich zur Leier.

Part One
XVII

At the bottom,
the ancient one,
tangled root of all that has been,
forgotten fountain left unseen.

Helmets and hunters' horns,
old men muttering,
brothers betrayed,
women played upon.

Branch thrusts upon branch,
nowhere a free one.
Yes, up there! Keep climbing!

See if they'll hold you.
That high one bends already
to become a lyre.

Hörst du das Neue, Herr,
dröhnen und beben?
Kommen Verkündiger,
die es erheben.

Zwar ist kein Hören heil
in dem Durchtobtsein,
doch der Maschinenteil
will jetzt gelobt sein.

Sieh, die Maschine:
wie sie sich wälzt und rächt
und uns entstellt und schwächt.

Hat sie aus uns auch Kraft,
sie, ohne Leidenschaft,
treibe und diene.

Part One
XVIII

Orpheus, do you hear
the new sound,
droning and roaring?
Many now exult in it.

Though the (Machine)
insists on our praise,
who can listen
with all this noise?

evil of technology

See, it rolls over everything,
weakening us
and taking our place.

Since its strength is of our making,
why can't it serve
and not possess us?

Erster Teil
XIX

Wandelt sich rasch auch die Welt
wie Wolkengestalten,
alles Vollendete fällt
heim zum Uralten.

Über dem Wandel und Gang,
weiter und freier,
währt noch dein Vor-Gesang,
Gott mit der Leier.

Nicht sind die Leiden erkannt,
nicht ist die Liebe gelernt,
und was im Tod uns entfernt,

ist nicht entschleiert.
Einzig das Lied überm Land
heiligt und feiert.

Part One
XIX

As swiftly as the world is changing,
like racing clouds,
all that is finished
falls home to the ancient source.

Above the change and the loss,
farther and freer,
your singing continues,
god of the lyre.

How can we embrace our sorrows
or learn how to love,
or see what we lose

when we die? Only your song
over the earth
honors our life and makes it holy.

Dir aber, Herr, o was weih ich dir, sag,
der das Ohr den Geschöpfen gelehrt?—
Mein Erinnern an einen Frühlingstag,
seinen Abend, in Rußland—, ein Pferd . . .

Herüber vom Dorf kam der Schimmel allein,
an der vorderen Fessel den Pflock,
um die Nacht auf den Wiesen allein zu sein;
wie schlug seiner Mähne Gelock

an den Hals im Takte des Übermuts,
bei dem grob gehemmten Galopp.
Wie sprangen die Quellen des Rossebluts!

Der fühlte die Weiten, und ob!
Der sang und der hörte—, dein Sagenkreis
war *in* ihm geschlossen. Sein Bild: ich weih's.

Part One
XX

Tell me, Orpheus, what offering can I make
to you, who taught the creatures how to listen?
I remember a spring day in Russia;
it was evening, and a horse . . .

He came up from the village, a gray horse, alone.
With a hobble attached to one leg
he headed to the fields for the night.
How the thick mane beat against his neck

in rhythm with his high spirits
and his impeded, lurching gallop.
How all that was horse in him quickened.

He embraced the distances as if he could sing them,
as if your songs were completed in him.
His image is my offering.

Frühling ist wiedergekommen. Die Erde
ist wie ein Kind, das Gedichte weiß;
viele, o viele . . . Für die Beschwerde
langen Lernens bekommt sie den Preis.

Streng war ihr Lehrer. Wir mochten das Weiße
an dem Barte des alten Manns.
Nun, wie das Grüne, das Blaue heiße,
dürfen wir fragen: sie kanns, sie kanns!

Erde, die frei hat, du glückliche, spiele
nun mit den Kindern. Wir wollen dich fangen,
fröhliche Erde. Dem Frohsten gelingts.

O, was der Lehrer sie lehrte, das Viele,
und was gedruckt steht in Wurzeln und langen
schwierigen Stammen: sie singts, sie singts!

Part One
XXI

Spring! And Earth is like a child
who has learned many poems by heart.
For the trouble of that long learning
she wins the prize.

Her teacher was strict. We loved the white
of the old man's beard. Now we can ask her
the many names of green, of blue,
and she knows them, she knows them!

Earth, school is out now. You're free
to play with the children. We'll catch you,
joyous Earth. The happiest will catch you!

All that the teacher taught her—the many thoughts
pressed now into roots and long
tough stems: she sings! She sings!

Erster Teil
XXII

Wir sind die Treibenden.
Aber den Schritt der Zeit,
nehmt ihn als Kleinigkeit
im immer Bleibenden.

Alles das Eilende
wird schon vorüber sein;
denn das Verweilende
erst weiht uns ein.

Knaben, o werft den Mut
nicht in die Schnelligkeit,
nicht in den Flugversuch.

Alles ist ausgeruht:
Dunkel und Helligkeit,
Blume und Buch.

Part One
XXII

We set the pace.
But this press of time—
take it as a little thing
next to what endures.

All this hurrying
soon will be over.
Only when we tarry
do we touch the holy.

Young ones, don't waste your courage
racing so fast,
flying so high.

See how all things are at rest—
darkness and morning light,
blossom and book.

Sollen wir unsere uralte Freundschaft, die großen
niemals werbenden Götter, weil sie der harte
Stahl, den wir streng erzogen, nicht kennt, verstoßen
oder sie plötzlich suchen auf einer Karte?

Diese gewaltigen Freunde, die uns die Toten
nehmen, rühren nirgends an unsere Räder.
Unsere Gastmähler haben wir weit——, unsere Bäder,
fortgerückt, und ihre uns lang schon zu langsamen Boten

überholen wir immer. Einsamer nun aufeinander
ganz angewiesen, ohne einander zu kennen,
führen wir nicht mehr die Pfade als schöne Mäander,

sondern als Grade. Nur noch in Dampfkesseln brennen
die einstigen Feuer und heben die Hämmer, die immer
größern. Wir aber nehmen an Kraft ab, wie Schwimmer.

Part One
XXIV

Our oldest friends—the great gods
who never tried to woo us—
shall we reject them because our tools of steel
do not need them? Or shall we seek them on a map?

Those powerful friends, who receive our dead,
play no part in our wheels and gears.
We have moved our banquets far from them,
and pass their messengers with such speed

we can't hear what they say. Lonelier now,
having no one but each other, not knowing each other,
we no longer meander on curving paths, but race straight
        ahead.

Only in the mills do the once sacred fires still burn,
lifting ever heavier hammers, while we
diminish in strength, like swimmers at sea.

Erster Teil
XXV

Dich aber will ich nun, *Dich,* die ich kannte
wie eine Blume, von der ich den Namen nicht weiß,
noch *ein* Mal erinnern und ihnen zeigen, Entwandte,
schöne Gespielin des unüberwindlichen Schrei's.

Tänzerin erst, die plötzlich, den Körper voll Zögern,
anhielt, als göß man ihr Jungsein in Erz;
trauernd und lauschend—. Da, von den hohen Vermögern
fiel ihr Musik in das veränderte Herz.

Nah war die Krankheit. Schon von den Schatten bemächtigt,
drängte verdunkelt das Blut, doch, wie flüchtig verdächtigt,
trieb es in seinen natürlichen Frühling hervor.

Wieder und wieder, von Dunkel und Sturz unterbrochen,
glänzte es irdisch. Bis es nach schrecklichen Pochen
trat in das trostlos offene Tor.

Part One
XXV

It's you, dear Wera, I would remember now,
like a flower I knew before I could name it.
I would show you to the gods,
you vanished one, you unforgotten cry.

Dancer before all else, you hesitated,
paused, as if your youth could be cast in bronze.
Bringing grief and a strange attention,
your music changed the heart.

Then the illness came. Shadows gathered,
a darkness in the blood,
cutting short your springtime.

And, as if your dancing
were a knocking at the door,
it opened, and you entered.

Du aber, Göttlicher, du, bis zuletzt noch Ertöner,
da ihn der Schwarm der verschmähten Mänaden befiel,
hast ihr Geschrei übertönt mit Ordnung, du Schöner,
aus den Zerstörenden stieg dein erbauendes Spiel.

Keine war da, daß sie Haupt dir und Leier zerstör.
Wie sie auch rangen und rasten, und alle die scharfen
Steine, die sie nach deinem Herzen warfen,
wurden zu Sanftem an dir und begabt mit Gehör.

Schließlich zerschlugen sie dich, von der Rache gehetzt,
während dein Klang noch in Löwen und Felsen verweilte
und in den Bäumen und Vögeln. Dort singst du noch jetzt.

O du verlorener Gott! Du unendliche Spur!
Nur weil dich reißend zuletzt die Feindschaft verteilte,
sind wir die Hörenden jetzt und ein Mund der Natur.

Part One
XXVI

But you, divine poet, to the end a singer:
falling prey to the pack of Maenads,
you wove their shrieking into wider harmonies,
and brought from that destruction a song to build with.

No one to call when they raged and wrestled,
but the jagged stones they hurled
turned gentle when reaching you,
as if able to hear you.

Hounded by hatred, you were torn to pieces
while your music still rang amidst rocks and lions,
trees and birds. There you are singing still.

O dear lost god, you endless path!
Only because you were broken and scattered
have we become the ears of nature, and her voice.

Zweiter Teil

I

Atmen, du unsichtbares Gedicht!
Immerfort um das eigne
Sein rein eingetauschter Weltraum. Gegengewicht,
in dem ich mich rhythmisch ereigne.

Einzige Welle, deren
allmähliches Meer ich bin;
sparsamstes du von allen möglichen Meeren,—
Raumgewinn.

Wieviele von diesen Stellen der Räume waren schon
innen in mir. Manche Winde
sind wie mein Sohn.

Erkennst du mich, Luft, du, voll noch einst meiniger Orte?
Du, einmal glatte Rinde,
Rundung und Blatt meiner Worte.

Part Two
I

Breath, you invisible poem!
Pure, continuous exchange
with all that is, flow and counterflow
where rhythmically I come to be.

Each time a wave that occurs just once
in a sea I discover I am.
You, innermost of oceans,
you, infinitude of space.

How many far places were once
within me. Some winds
are like my own child.

When I breathe them now, do they know me again?
Air, you silken surround,
completion and seed of my words.

O dieses ist das Tier, das es nicht gibt.
Sie wußtens nicht und habens jeden Falls
—sein Wandeln, seine Haltung, seinen Hals,
bis in des stillen Blickes Licht—geliebt.

Zwar *war* es nicht. Doch weil sie's liebten, ward
ein reines Tier. Sie ließen immer Raum.
Und in dem Raume, klar und ausgespart,
erhob es leicht sein Haupt und brauchte kaum

zu sein. Sie nährten es mit keinem Korn,
nur immer mit der Möglichkeit, es sei.
Und die gab solche Stärke an das Tier,

daß es aus sich ein Stirnhorn trieb. Ein Horn.
Zu einer Jungfrau kam es weiß herbei—
und war im Silber-Spiegel und in ihr.

Part Two
IV

This is the animal that never was.
They didn't know, and loved him anyway:
his bearing, his neck, the way he moved,
the light in his quiet eyes.

True, he didn't exist. But because they loved him
he became a real animal. They made a space for him.
And in that clear, uncluttered space he lifted his head
and hardly needed to exist.

They fed him: not with grain, but ever
with the chance that he could be.
And that so strengthened him

that, from within, he grew a horn.
All white, he drew near to a virgin and found himself
in a silver mirror and in her.

Zweiter Teil
VIII

Wenige ihr, der einstigen Kindheit Gespielen
in den zerstreuten Gärten der Stadt:
wie wir uns fanden und uns zögernd gefielen
und, wie das Lamm mit dem redenden Blatt,

sprachen als Schweigende. Wenn wir uns einmal freuten,
keinem gehörte es. Wessen wars?
Und wie zergings unter allen den gehenden Leuten
und im Bangen des langen Jahrs.

Wagen umrollten uns fremd, vorübergezogen,
Häuser umstanden uns stark, aber unwahr,—und keines
kannte uns je. *Was* war wirklich im All?

Nichts. Nur die Bälle. Ihre herrlichen Bogen.
Auch nicht die Kinder . . . Aber manchmal trat eines,
ach ein vergehendes, unter den fallenden Ball.

In memoriam Egon von Rilke

Part Two
VIII

There were a few of us, playmates
in the scattered gardens of the city.
Remember how we found each other
and hesitantly liked each other,

and, like the lamb with the talking scroll,
spoke in silences. The good times we had belonged to
   no one.
Whose could they be? They disappeared amid all the
   hurrying people
and the worries to come with the long years.

Wagons and trucks rolled by. We didn't care.
Houses rose around us, solid but unreal, and no one knew us.
What, after all, *was* real?

Nothing. Only the ball, the beautiful arcs it made.
Not even the children were real, except for that moment
of reaching up and ah! catching the ball.

Rühmt euch, ihr Richtenden, nicht der entbehrlichen Folter
und daß das Eisen nicht länger an Hälsen sperrt.
Keins ist gesteigert, kein Herz—, weil ein gewollter
Krampf der Milde euch zarter verzerrt.

Was es durch Zeiten bekam, das schenkt das Schafott
wieder zurück, wie Kinder ihr Spielzeug vom vorig
alten Geburtstag. Ins reine, ins hohe, ins thorig
offene Herz träte er anders, der Gott

wirklicher Milde. Er käme gewaltig und griffe
strahlender um sich, wie Göttliche sind.
Mehr als ein Wind für die großen gesicherten Schiffe.

Weniger nicht, als die heimliche leise Gewahrung,
die uns im Innern schweigend gewinnt
wie ein still spielendes Kind aus unendlicher Paarung.

Part Two
IX

Don't boast, you judges, that you no longer torture
or clamp an iron collar 'round the neck.
Though the mercy we longed for
may rearrange your features

and the scaffold fall into disuse
like an outgrown toy,
no one is better off.
The god of true mercy would step differently

into the undefended heart.
He would enter with radiance
the way gods do, strong as the sea wind

for treasure-bearing ships, and claim us as lightly
as the child of an infinite union
absorbed in play.

Zweiter Teil
X

Alles Erworbne bedroht die Maschine, solange
sie sich erdreistet, im Geist, statt im Gehorchen, zu sein.
Daß nicht der herrlichen Hand schöneres Zögern mehr prange,
zu dem entschlossenern Bau schneidet sie steifer den Stein.

Nirgends bleibt sie zurück, daß wir ihr *ein* Mal entrönnen
und sie in stiller Fabrik ölend sich selber gehört.
Sie ist das Leben,—sie meint es am besten zu können,
die mit dem gleichen Entschluß ordnet und schafft und
    zerstört.

Aber noch ist uns das Dasein verzaubert; an hundert
Stellen ist es noch Ursprung. Ein Spielen von reinen
Kräften, die keiner berührt, der nicht kniet und bewundert.

Worte gehen noch zart am Unsäglichen aus . . .
Und die Musik, immer neu, aus den bebendsten Steinen,
baut im unbrauchbaren Raum ihr vergöttlichtes Haus.

Part Two
X

The Machine endangers all we have made.
We allow it to rule instead of obey.
To build a house, cut the stone sharp and fast:
the carver's hand takes too long to feel its way.

The Machine never hesitates, or we might escape
and its factories subside into silence.
It thinks it's alive and does everything better.
With equal resolve it creates and destroys.

But life holds mystery for us yet. In a hundred places
we can still sense the source: a play of pure powers
that—when you feel it—brings you to your knees.

There are yet words that come near the unsayable,
and, from crumbling stones, a new music
to make a sacred dwelling in a place we cannot own.

Wolle die Wandlung. O sei für die Flamme begeistert,
drin sich ein Ding dir entzieht, das mit Verwandlungen
     prunkt;
jener entwerfende Geist, welcher das Irdische meistert,
liebt in dem Schwung der Figur nichts wie den wendenden
     Punkt.

Was sich ins Bleiben verschließt, schon *ists* das Erstarrte;
wähnt es sich sicher im Schutz des unscheinbaren Grau's?
Warte, ein Härtestes warnt aus der Ferne das Harte.
Wehe—: abwesender Hammer holt aus!

Wer sich als Quelle ergießt, den erkennt die Erkennung;
und sie fuhrt ihn entzückt durch das heiter Geschaffne,
das mit Anfang oft schließt und mit Ende beginnt.

Jeder glückliche Raum ist Kind oder Enkel von Trennung,
den sie staunend durchgehn. Und die verwandelte Daphne
will, seit sie lorbeern fühlt, daß du dich wandelst in Wind.

Part Two
XII

Want the change. Be inspired by the flame
where everything shines as it disappears.
The artist, when sketching, loves nothing so much
as the curve of the body as it turns away.

What locks itself in sameness has congealed.
Is it safer to be gray and numb?
What turns hard becomes rigid
and is easily shattered.

Pour yourself out like a fountain.
Flow into the knowledge that what you are seeking
finishes often at the start, and, with ending, begins.

Every happiness is the child of a separation
it did not think it could survive. And Daphne, becoming
     a laurel,
dares you to become the wind.

Zweiter Teil
XIII

Sei allem Abschied voran, als wäre er hinter
dir, wie der Winter, der eben geht.
Denn unter Wintern ist einer so endlos Winter,
daß, überwinternd, dein Herz überhaupt übersteht.

Sei immer tot in Eurydike—, singender steige,
preisender steige zurück in den reinen Bezug.
Hier, unter Schwindenden, sei, im Reiche der Neige,
sei ein klingendes Glas, das sich im Klang schon zerschlug.

Sei—und wisse zugleich des Nicht-Seins Bedingung,
den unendlichen Grund deiner innigen Schwingung,
daß du sie völlig vollziehst dieses einzige Mal.

Zu dem gebrauchten sowohl, wie zum dumpfen und
    stummen
Vorrat der vollen Natur, den unsäglichen Summen,
zähle dich jubelnd hinzu und vernichte die Zahl.

Part Two
XIII

Be ahead of all parting, as if it had already happened,
like winter, which even now is passing.
For beneath the winter is a winter so endless
that to survive it at all is a triumph of the heart.

Be forever dead in Eurydice, and climb back singing.
Climb praising as you return to connection.
Here among the disappearing, in the realm of the transient,
be a ringing glass that shatters as it rings.

Be. And, at the same time, know what it is *not* to be.
That emptiness inside you allows you to vibrate
in resonance with your world. Use it for once.

To all that has run its course, and to the vast unsayable
numbers of beings abounding in Nature,
add yourself gladly, and cancel the cost.

Siehe die Blumen, diese dem Irdischen treuen,
denen wir Schicksal vom Rande des Schicksals leihn,—
aber wer weiß es! Wenn sie ihr Welken bereuen,
ist es an uns, ihre Reue zu sein.

Alles will schweben. Da gehn wir umher wie Beschwerer,
legen auf alles uns selbst, vom Gewichte entzückt;
o was sind wir den Dingen für zehrende Lehrer,
weil ihnen ewige Kindheit glückt.

Nähme sie einer ins innige Schlafen und schliefe
tief mit den Dingen—: o wie käme er leicht,
anders zum anderen Tag, aus der gemeinsamen Tiefe.

Oder er bliebe vielleicht; und sie blühten und priesen
ihn, den Bekehrten, der nun den Ihrigen gleicht,
allen den stillen Geschwistern im Winde der Wiesen.

Part Two
XIV

See the flowers, so faithful to Earth.
We know their fate because we share it.
Were they to grieve for their wilting,
that grief would be ours to feel.

There's a lightness in things. Only *we* move forever
    burdened,
pressing ourselves onto everything, obsessed by weight.
How strange and devouring our ways must seem
to those for whom life is enough.

If you could enter their dreaming and dream with them
    deeply,
you would come back different to a different day,
moving so easily from that common depth.

Or maybe just stay there: they would bloom and
    welcome you,
all those brothers and sisters tossing in the meadows,
and you would be one of them.

Zweiter Teil
XIX

Irgendwo wohnt das Gold in der verwöhnenden Bank
und mit Tausenden tut es vertraulich. Doch jener
Blinde, der Bettler, ist selbst dem kupfernen Zehner
wie ein verlorener Ort, wie das staubige Eck unterm
    Schrank.

In den Geschäften entlang ist das Geld wie zuhause
und verkleidet sich scheinbar in Seide, Nelken und Pelz.
Er, der Schweigende, steht in der Atempause
alles des wach oder schlafend atmenden Gelds.

O wie mag sie sich schließen bei Nacht, diese immer
    offene Hand.
Morgen holt sie das Schicksal wieder, und täglich
hält es sie hin: hell, elend, unendlich zerstörbar.

Daß doch einer, ein Schauender, endlich ihren langen
    Bestand
staunend begriffe und rühmte. Nur dem Aufsingenden
    säglich.
Nur dem Göttlichen hörbar.

Part Two
XIX

Gold leads a pampered life, protected by banks,
on intimate terms with the best people.
The homeless beggar is no more than a lost coin
fallen behind the bookcase or in the dustpile under the bed.

In the finest shops, money is right at home,
loving to parade itself in flowers, silk, and furs.
He, the silent one, stands outside this display.
Money, near him, stops breathing.

How does his outstretched hand ever close at night?
Fate, each morning, picks it up again,
holds it out there, naked and raw.

In order to grasp what his life is like,
to see it and cherish it, you would need a song,
a song only a god could bear to hear.

Zweiter Teil
XX

Zwischen den Sternen, wie weit; und doch, um wievieles
    noch weiter,
was man am Hiesigen lernt.
Einer, zum Beispiel, ein Kind . . . und ein Nächster,
    ein Zweiter—,
o wie unfaßlich entfernt.

Schicksal, es mißt uns vielleicht mit des Seienden Spanne,
daß es uns fremd erscheint;
denk, wieviel Spannen allein vom Mädchen zum Manne,
wenn es ihn meidet und meint.

Alles ist weit—, und nirgends schließt sich der Kreis.
Sieh in der Schüssel, auf heiter bereitetem Tische,
seltsam der Fische Gesicht.

Fische sind stumm . . . , meinte man einmal. Wer weiß?
Aber ist nicht am Ende ein Ort, wo man das, was der Fische
Sprache wäre, *ohne* sie spricht?

Part Two
XX

How far it is between the stars, and how much farther
is what's right here. The distance, for example,
between a child and one who walks by—
oh, how inconceivably far.

Not only in measurable spans does Fate
move through our lives.
Think how great the distance between a young girl
and the boy she avoids and loves.

Everything is far, nowhere does the circle close.
See, on the plate upon the festive table
how strangely the fish is staring.

Fish are mute, we used to think. Who knows?
We may, in the end, find that their silence
says more to us than our words.

XXI

Singe die Gärten, mein Herz, die du nicht kennst; wie in Glas
eingegossene Gärten, klar, unerreichbar.
Wasser und Rosen von Ispahan oder Schiras,
singe sie selig, preise sie, keinem vergleichbar.

Zeige, mein Herz, daß du sie niemals entbehrst.
Daß sie dich meinen, ihre reifenden Feigen.
Daß du mit ihren, zwischen den blühenden Zweigen
wie zum Gesicht gesteigerten Lüften verkehrst.

Meide den Irrtum, daß es Entbehrungen gebe
für den geschehnen Entschluß, diesen: zu sein!
Seidener Faden, kamst du hinein ins Gewebe.

Welchem der Bilder du auch im Innern geeint bist
(sei es selbst ein Moment aus dem Leben der Pein),
fühl, daß der ganze, der rühmliche Teppich gemeint ist.

Part Two
XXI

Sing, my heart, the gardens you never walked,
like gardens sealed in glass balls, unreachable.
Sing the waters and roses of Isfahan and Shiraz;
praise them, lush beyond compare.

Swear, my heart, that you will never give them up.
That the figs they ripened ripened for you.
That you could tell by its fragrance
each blossoming branch.

Don't imagine you could ever let them go
once they made the daring choice: to be!
Like a silken thread, you entered the weaving.

Whatever image you take within you deeply,
even for a moment in a lifetime of pain,
see how it reveals the whole—the great tapestry.

Zweiter Teil
XXII

O trotz Schicksal: die herrlichen Überflüsse
unseres Daseins, in Parken übergeschäumt,—
oder als steinerne Männer neben die Schlüsse
hoher Portale, unter Balkone gebäumt!

O die eherne Glocke, die ihre Keule
täglich wider den stumpfen Alltag hebt.
Oder die *eine,* in Karnak, die Säule,
die Säule, die fast ewige Tempel überlebt.

Heute stürzen die Überschüsse, dieselben,
nur noch als Eile vorbei, aus dem waagrechten gelben
Tag in die blendend mit Licht übertriebene Nacht.

Aber das Rasen zergeht und läßt keine Spuren.
Kurven des Flugs durch die Luft und die, die sie fuhren,
keine vielleicht ist umsonst. Doch nur wie gedacht.

Part Two
XXII

In spite of Fate, the marvelous abundance
of being, like the brimming land
or like stone figures
built into gateways, bearing up balconies.

Or a bronze bell, lifting its voice
over and over against the dullness of our days.
Or that single column in Karnak, standing
long after the temple fell.

Today this extravagance flashes by
in the blur of our haste,
out of the wide yellow day into the vaulted night.

In that rush it dissolves, leaving nothing behind,
just as a plane overhead makes no mark on the sky.
Only our minds see the curve of its flight.

Zweiter Teil
XXIV

O diese Lust, immer neu, aus gelockertem Lehm!
Niemand beinah hat den frühesten Wagern geholfen.
Städte entstanden trotzdem an beseligten Golfen,
Wasser und Öl füllten die Krüge trotzdem.

Götter, wir planen sie erst in erkühnten Entwürfen,
die uns das mürrische Schicksal wieder zerstört.
Aber sie sind die Unsterblichen. Sehet, wir dürfen
jenen erhorchen, der uns am Ende erhört.

Wir, ein Geschlecht durch Jahrtausende: Mütter und Väter,
immer erfüllter von dem künftigen Kind,
daß es uns einst, übersteigend, erschüttere, später.

Wir, wir unendlich Gewagten, was haben wir Zeit!
Und nur der schweigsame Tod, der weiß, was wir sind
und was er immer gewinnt, wenn er uns leiht.

Part Two
XXIV

Oh, the pleasure of it, always emerging new
from the loosened clay. Those who dared to come first
had hardly any help. Nevertheless cities arose
on sun-favored coasts, and pitchers filled with water and oil.

Gods: we picture them first in wild brushstrokes
which petty Fate keeps wiping away.
But gods don't die. Let us listen to them;
they will be there to hear us at the end.

We are one generation through thousands of years,
mothers and fathers shaped by children to come,
who, in their turn, will overtake them.

We are endlessly offered into life: all time is ours.
And what any one of us might be worth,
death alone knows—and does not tell.

Gibt es wirklich die Zeit, die zerstörende?
Wann, auf dem ruhenden Berg, zerbricht sie die Burg?
Dieses Herz, das unendlich den Göttern gehörende,
wann vergewaltigts der Demiurg?

Sind wir wirklich so ängstlich Zerbrechliche,
wie das Schicksal uns wahr machen will?
Ist die Kindheit, die tiefe, versprechliche,
in den Wurzeln—später—still?

Ach, das Gespenst des Vergänglichen,
durch den arglos Empfänglichen
geht es, als wär es ein Rauch.

Als die, die wir sind, als die Treibenden,
gelten wir doch bei bleibenden
Kräften als göttlicher Brauch.

Part Two
XXVII

Does Time, as it passes, really destroy?
It may rip the fortress from its rock;
but can this heart, that belongs to God,
be torn from Him by circumstance?

Are we as fearfully fragile
as Fate would have us believe?
Can we ever be severed
from childhood's deep promise?

Ah, the knowledge of impermanence
that haunts our days
is their very fragrance.

We in our striving think we should last forever,
but could we be used by the Divine
if we were not ephemeral?

Zweiter Teil
XXIX

Stiller Freund der vielen Fernen, fühle,
wie dein Atem noch den Raum vermehrt.
Im Gebälk der finstern Glockenstühle
laß dich läuten. Das, was an dir zehrt,

wird ein Starkes über dieser Nahrung.
Geh in der Verwandlung aus und ein.
Was ist deine leidendste Erfahrung?
Ist dir Trinken bitter, werde Wein.

Sei in dieser Nacht aus Übermaß
Zauberkraft am Kreuzweg deiner Sinne,
ihrer seltsamen Begegnung Sinn.

Und wenn dich das Irdische vergaß,
zu der stillen Erde sag: Ich rinne.
Zu dem raschen Wasser sprich: Ich bin.

Part Two
XXIX

Quiet friend who has come so far,
feel how your breathing makes more space around you.
Let this darkness be a bell tower
and you the bell. As you ring,

what batters you becomes your strength.
Move back and forth into the change.
What is it like, such intensity of pain?
If the drink is bitter, turn yourself to wine.

In this uncontainable night,
be the mystery at the crossroads of your senses,
the meaning discovered there.

And if the world has ceased to hear you,
say to the silent earth: I flow.
To the rushing water, speak: I am.

NOTES

DUINO ELEGIES

THE FIRST ELEGY

ll. 1ff. *If I cried out:* The words of this first question came to
Rilke on January 20, 1912, resounding in his mind as he walked in a
strong wind on a footpath overlooking the Adriatic Sea. He was
staying alone at Duino Castle, a guest of his patron, Princess Marie
von Thurn und Taxis. As he described in a letter to her, the
Duino Elegies began in this moment. The first was completed in
a single day.

Earlier that very day, Rilke had received two letters. One, from
his lawyer, pertained to financial obligations in his separation from
Clara Westhoff. The other, from Viktor von Gebsattel, replied to
Rilke's query about the advisability of embarking on a psycho-
analytic treatment with him. Plagued by depression, hypochon-
dria, and writer's block, the poet was torn between the benefits and
the losses he imagined treatment might bring him. Gebsattel's
letter, now evidently lost, seems to have reinforced Rilke's hesita-
tions to think of his anguish as a pathology and his inclinations to

brave it as a potential source of creativity. In any case, the poet appears ready now to endure his own pain and trust his own outcry, even when there is no one—no angel, no person—capable of truly hearing it.

l. 7. *For beauty is but the beginning of terror:* A dozen years earlier, in *The Book of Hours,* Rilke sensed that inevitable connection: "Let everything happen to you: beauty and terror" (I, 59).

l. 27. *For whom is night not there?* See *Rilke's Book of Hours,* I, 11: "You, darkness, of whom I am born— / I love you more than the flame / that limits the world / to the circle it illumines / and excludes all the rest . . . I believe in the night."

ll. 38–39. *Springtimes have needed you:* Rilke reiterates the bold sense of reciprocity that informs *The Book of Hours* from the very first poem: "I know that nothing has ever been real / without my beholding it. / All becoming has needed me" (I, 1).

l. 48. *Let yourself feel it, that yearning:* Rilke's counsel is comparable to mindfulness practice in Buddhism, where attention is directed to the immediate sensation rather than to the stories we make up about it.

l. 59. *For there is nowhere to remain:* We are reminded of the description of the bodhisattva. The early scriptures present this hero figure of the Buddhist tradition as being so attuned to the impermanence of all things that he or she has nowhere to abide: "Like a rain-bearing cloud, he has no place to settle down, nor anywhere to stand"; "Like a bird riding on the wind, the bodhisattva goes forth, does not remain anywhere, but stands on wisdom only" (*The Perfection of Wisdom in Eight Thousand Lines,* pp. 59, 91).

THE SECOND ELEGY

ll. 1–8. *Any angel is frightening:* As in the First Elegy, angels are presented as dangerous because they embody a seductive perfection untouched by time.

ll. 10–17. *Fated to be happy:* These archetypal figures now are viewed as pitiful and even repulsive. They seem almost stagnant in their exalted changelessness. In this respect, angels serve as a foil to allow our own moment-by-moment mortality to emerge more nakedly in the lines that follow.

ll. 37–46. *Does the universe we dissolve into:* Our impermanence comes as a necessary condition in an interdependent universe. This causal reciprocity was conveyed earlier in many poems in *The Book of Hours,* for example: "What will you do, God, when I die?" (I, 36); "On the day you made us you created yourself" (I, 25); "I am the dream you are dreaming" (I, 19).

ll. 74ff. *You touch one another so reverently:* Lovers are seen as the true knowers of impermanence, as in *The Book of Hours*: "They are the poets of one brief hour. / They kiss an expressionless mouth into a smile / as if creating it anew, more beautiful" (II, 10).

THE EIGHTH ELEGY

The Austrian writer Rudolf Kassner was a good and lifelong friend of Rilke's.

By "the Open," a term rarely used elsewhere in his poetry, Rilke seems to mean the phenomenal world uncontaminated by our ideas about it. Beholding it requires a nondualistic consciousness, a mind that does not objectify reality with concepts and comparisons. In a letter written shortly before his death in 1926, Rilke took pains to distinguish the Open from any aspect of perceived reality:

"By the 'Open' it is not sky or air or space that is meant; they too, for the human being who observes and judges, are 'objects' and thus 'opaque' and closed. The animal or the flower presumably *is* all that without accounting for itself."

As far as we know, animals do not dwell in advance on their own dying; so, in a sense, their death has already happened for them. As Rilke wrote in *The Book of Hours*: "Lord, we are more wretched than the animals / who do their dying once and for all, / for we are never finished with our not dying" (III, 8).

Rilke did use the term "the Open" in reference to his own death. He instructed his friends: "Any clerical go-between would be an insult and an impediment to the movement of my soul toward the Open" (Prater, p. 383).

THE NINTH ELEGY

l. 2. *as laurel, say:* The laurel refers to Daphne, who was pursued by Apollo and was turned into a laurel tree to escape him. See Sonnets to Orpheus, Part Two, XII, where Daphne also appears as a challenge to us to allow ourselves to change.

ll. 32ff. *Could we be here, then, / in order to say:* See *Rilke's Book of Hours*, I, 60: "I want, then, simply / to say the names of things."

l. 64. *Praise the world to the angel:* As if shifting into a major key, Rilke summons us to extol life. Here themes of impermanence and gratitude join strongly, as they do implicitly throughout the Sonnets.

l. 66. *In the universe, where he feels feelings:* Ten years after the First and Second Elegies, the angel is friendlier, and capable of emotion.

l. 83. *Earth, isn't this what you want?* Rilke speaks directly to the earth, as he did in *The Book of Hours*: "Dear darkening ground, / you've endured so patiently the walls we've built" (I, 61). There he addressed the earth as a sacred object of worship; here it is addressed as a lover.

SONNETS TO ORPHEUS

PART ONE, SONNET I

l. 1. *A tree rose there:* The upward thrust of the tree reflects the surge of inspiration Rilke is experiencing as the ten-year drought is broken. A similar image is found frequently in *The Book of Hours*, where it denotes creative energy and a kind of resurrection:

> *Such is the amazing play of the powers:*
> *they give themselves so willingly,*
> *swelling in the roots, thinning as the trunks rise,*
> *and in the high leaves, resurrection. [I, 22]*

> *the deep one, whose being I trust,*
> *for it breaks through the earth into trees . . . [II, 3]*

> *If we surrendered*
> *to earth's intelligence*
> *we could rise up rooted, like trees. [II, 16]*

l. 2. *Now I can hear the tree:* The original German places the tree in the poet's ear, and it has generally been translated thus. We found that image distracting and uncomfortable.

PART ONE, SONNET II

The girl in question is Wera Ouckama Knoop, the recently deceased daughter of Munich friends. Rilke had learned of her death the month before writing the Sonnets, and although he had known her only briefly, he would dedicate to her the entire work. Reading these lines, we wonder whether she might not in some measure represent for Rilke his own poetic gift. His creativity had slept in him while containing all the things he had loved.

l. 4. *She became inseparable from my own hearing:* The original line translates literally, "and she made herself a bed in my ear." As in the previous sonnet, we have done Rilke the favor of removing objects from his ear.

PART ONE, SONNET III

l. 4. *temple for Apollo:* Orpheus was a devotee of Apollo, from whom he received his lyre.

ll. 5–6. *Song, as you teach us:* The poet may be speaking wisdom learned during his ten years of meager inspiration. The song cannot be produced by effort or willpower or even the intoxication of passion; it is an expression of being.

PART ONE, SONNET IV

l. 1. *enter the breathing:* Breath as a rhythmic reality and as a metaphor runs through many of the Sonnets. Its significance is threefold: it expresses our ephemerality; it physically connects us with the natural world; and it helps us release our grasping. Breath seems to exist independently of us, like a pulse of the universe.

l. 9ff. *Fear not the pain:* Our pain, if not denied or avoided, can reconnect us to the larger world. In *The Book of Hours,* Rilke says:

Be earth now, and evensong.
Be the ground lying under that sky. [II, 1]

This is what the things can teach us:
to fall,
patiently to trust our heaviness.
Even a bird has to do that
before he can fly. [II, 16]

Here heaviness turns our pain to belonging.

PART ONE, SONNET V

This may be read as a hymn to impermanence, of which Orpheus is both symbol and teacher.

l. 1. *Just let the rose:* Ever the emblem of living beauty in all its fragility, the rose was beloved of Rilke when he lived in the Valais. In his last years, after the completion of the Sonnets and the Elegies, he wrote a collection of twenty-four rose poems in French and cultivated a rose garden at Muzot.

J. R. von Salis, in *Rainer Maria Rilke: The Years in Switzerland,* recounts: "There was a rosebed in the Muzot garden. Rilke cared for the roses like a gardener, watering and pruning them with his own hands. Like everything he did, it was done with love. The garden, the roses, returned this love. For their sake he kept going back to Muzot. When he was out of tune with himself, suffering and ill, and nothing else could help him, he found consolation in his roses."

The rose is invoked also on Rilke's gravestone:

Rose, oh reiner Widerspruch, Lust
Niemandes Schlaf zu sein unter soviel Lidern.

Rose, o pure contradiction,
The joy of being no one's sleep under so many eyelids.

Orpheus emerges as not just the singer of poetry, but also the fearless knower of death. Not only is death part of life; it is essential to seeing life—indeed, to the very act of seeing.

The image of the willow in two parts—one aboveground, the other invisible below—conveys Rilke's notion of the complementarity of death and life. In a letter written shortly after this poem, he used another image in a similar way: "As the moon, so life undoubtedly has a side permanently turned away from us which is not its opposite but its complement, to bring it to perfection, to the full count, to the truly whole sphere and roundness of existence. . . . Life's word is always Yes and No at the same time. But death . . . is the final Yes, says only Yes" (Prater, pp. 353–354).

PART ONE, SONNET VII

l. 1. *It is all about praising:* This statement of our essential vocation prefigures the Ninth Duino Elegy, which Rilke would complete in the week after he wrote this sonnet.

ll. 2–3. *his heart / is a winepress:* Rilke included an additional metaphor here, that Orpheus went forth like ore from the silence of stone. We have kept to the metaphor of the vineyard.

l. 7. *All becomes vineyard:* From Muzot, Rilke viewed the vineyards of the Valais, and he walked through them almost daily. These lines, which express his love for the region, could also be understood as describing himself. His heart is a winepress now, with the emergence of this great work, and he is ripening in the southland of his being.

PART ONE, SONNET IX

Once more, the double realm is evoked, the necessary presence of death in life. Having gone to fetch his wife, Orpheus brought back not Eurydice, but something yet more valuable and life-transforming. Now his music is so clear that even the softest tone is heard, and his voice carries all he would say.

PART ONE, SONNET XI

As elsewhere, Rilke touches on opposites and apparent contradictions, and shows how illuminating it is to see them interact, whether it is rider and steed, or stars and the pictures we impose on them. He gracefully acknowledges our projections as ways in which we find meaning and perceive the beauty of the world.

PART ONE, SONNET XII

Imagination is required to see the world in terms of its connections. Relationships and the energies they generate are not discernible to the physical eye.

PART ONE, SONNET XIII

Impermanence allows life's generosity and the mysteries of transformation to be revealed in the most ordinary of acts.

PART ONE, SONNET XVII

The song seems to come from the tree itself, which now is like an *axis mundi,* connecting all eras and epochs. As we give ourselves to the climb and follow it upward, we find a lyre. Any of us can be Orpheus.

PART ONE, SONNET XVIII

This is the first of the Sonnets that rebel against the costs of industrialization. The Machine is presented in terms of sound, the modality of Orpheus. Its noise makes it difficult to hear his song.

Incidentally, we would have you know that when we translate, we work together with pencil and paper—no laptops around.

PART ONE, SONNET XIX

Impermanence is often portrayed by Rilke as a kind of falling, as in the poem "Autumn" from *The Book of Images*:

The leaves are falling, falling from so far,
as if distant gardens in the heavens were withering. . . .

And in the nights the heavy Earth is falling
from among the stars, into the loneliness.

We all are falling. This hand is falling.
And look around: it is in all of us. . . .

PART ONE, SONNET XX

Rilke is recalling a journey he made more than twenty years earlier with Lou Andreas-Salomé, the brilliant Russian-born woman who, once his lover, remained his lifelong friend. After composing this sonnet, Rilke wrote her that he had evoked "the carefree white horse hobbled by the fetlock that once came galloping to us just before evening in a meadow by the Volga."

In the recollected experience and in the poem itself, what carries particular weight is the image of the hobble impeding the horse's gait. The impediment itself heightens the freedom that the horse embodies.

PART ONE, SONNET XXI

Rilke's feeling for Earth partakes of the full range of devotion we find in world religions, expressing itself as gratitude for and cherishing of child and even lover, as well as for a parent.

Rarely, however, does the archetype of the Divine Child demonstrate such interactive playfulness, engaging us in a game of tag. And rarely does its sacredness appear compressed into organic form.

On February 9, 1922, Rilke wrote, "This little spring-song seems to me, as it were, an 'interpretation' of a remarkable dancing music that I once heard sung by the convent children at a morning Mass in the little church at Ronda [in southern Spain]. The children, who kept leaping to a dance rhythm, sang a text I didn't know, to the accompaniment of a triangle and tambourine" (Mitchell, *The Sonnets to Orpheus*, p. 120).

PART ONE, SONNET XXII

In the tempo of a lullaby comes this reminder that acceptance of impermanence does not imply a tolerance for haste. Transient as we are, there still is rest for us at the heart of things.

PART ONE, SONNET XXIV

The hurry that besets us, driven by technology, weakens us like swimmers at sea, and cuts us off from one another and from the sacred.

PART ONE, SONNET XXV

As we know, the Sonnets to Orpheus took form not long after Rilke received a letter from Wera Knoop's mother, describing her illness and death. Could it be that the death of this lovely young person served as a dramatic reminder of the poet's task? In the realm of mortality, the work of the poet is to cherish and remember.

PART ONE, SONNET XXVI

As mystery and wisdom traditions reveal, the experience of dismemberment helps assure the ongoingness of life. In this case, the redemption made possible by the dying god brings us an added gift: that of becoming the ears and the voice of nature. This gift is described in Part One, Sonnet I, where Orpheus awakened in the animals the yearning to hear and "made them, from their listening, a temple."

PART TWO, SONNET I

Readers today may be better prepared to appreciate this poem than readers in Rilke's day, because meditation practices that cultivate mindful breathing have become widespread.

PART TWO, SONNET IV

In referring to this sonnet, Rilke mentioned French medieval tapestries (Mitchell, *The Sonnets to Orpheus*, p. 173). "In the unicorn," he wrote, "no parallel with Christ is intended; rather, all love of the non-proven, the non-graspable, all belief in the value and reality of whatever our heart has through the centuries created and lifted out of itself: that is what is praised in this creature."

PART TWO, SONNET VIII

Rilke's note to this poem reads: "The lamb (in medieval paint-ings) which speaks only by means of a scroll with an inscription on it" (Mitchell, *The Selected Poetry of Rainer Maria Rilke*, p. 338).

In *The Book of Hours* as well as here, the ball that children toss and run to catch is a symbol of immediacy and pure attention. In the earlier work, Rilke playfully likens the ball to God:

I'd have tossed you into the ringing air
like a ball that someone leaps for and catches
with hands outstretched. [I, 21]

PART TWO, SONNET IX

We appreciate Rilke's realism, even though he could not have imagined the more sophisticated instruments of torture employed today. Justice and compassion involve more than cessation of their use. Radiance, sea wind, a child at play all suggest a grace beyond any political program.

PART TWO, SONNET X

The poet's indictment of industrial technology extends to its imprisoning and deadening effect on the human mind. A redeem-ing mystery, a play of pure powers, can still be found, as he reminded us some twenty years earlier in *The Book of Hours*:

Such is the amazing play of the powers:
they give themselves so willingly. [I, 22]

As in the first sonnet of Part One, music has the capacity to create a sacred place.

In October 1911, on his way to Duino Castle, Rilke was driven by Princess Marie's chauffeur for nine days through France and Italy. He wrote this to his friend and publisher Anton Kippenberg: "Not always easy, at each night's stop, to recover from the tempo and find myself again. The machine is in control, and you are its property; at night you lie in bed like a sort of spare part, your dreams and ideas those of a nut and bolt" (Prater, p. 196).

PART TWO, SONNET XII

Change is not just to be tolerated; it is to be desired. To continue in that spirit, we use the imperative (rather than the indicative of the original) in the first tercet.

In the Greek myth, the nymph Daphne ran from the pursuing Apollo and was turned into a laurel tree. Transformation is handy, even vital.

PART TWO, SONNET XIII

Orpheus, having descended into the Underworld to retrieve Eurydice, loses her on the return trip. Rilke tells him to climb back singing instead of grieving: he is to sing because he returns to a world that is alive and can hear him—he returns "to connection." Nevertheless, the knowledge of death remains strong within him. Orpheus dwells in a "double realm," the world of the living and, at the same time, the world of the dead. Rilke suggests that even in our daily life, awareness of not-being can accompany awareness of being. This twofold knowing, like sensing the winter beneath all winters, allows resonance and multidimensionality to arise. It brings truth to existence, and also permits abundance of generosity with oneself, one's life.

PART TWO, SONNET XIV

Our lives can be endlessly enriched not only by awareness of death but also by the company of our nonhuman kin. To "dream with them deeply" lets us return with greater resonance, as Orpheus did from the Underworld.

Rilke tends to use weight and gravity to suggest surrender into the life we share with Earth, as in this poem from *The Book of Hours*:

How surely gravity's law,
strong as an ocean current,
takes hold of even the smallest thing
and pulls it toward the heart of the world. [II, 16]

Here, by contrast, lightness is used to connote surrender. It allows us to move with the wind, to be buoyed by grace.

PART TWO, SONNET XIX

For this poet, the imperative to praise knows no limit. The life of a beggar deserves to be honored and sung, even if only a god can stand to hear it.

Early on, Rilke began to put into verse his regard for the poor. The third part of *The Book of Hours*, written in 1903, when he was twenty-six, is entitled *The Book of Poverty and Death*. In it, Rilke speaks as the poor:

Around us swirls the dust of the cities,
garbage clings to us.
We are shunned as if contaminated,
thrown away like broken pots, like bones,
like last year's calendar. [III, 16]

PART TWO, SONNET XX

We are often sermonized about our essential oneness or admonished to feel instant intimacy, and thus it is refreshing to be reminded of how vast is our not-knowing of one another.

PART TWO, SONNET XXI

The poet's praising is not limited to his own experience. He summons us to imagine the sensory presence of things—like the unicorn in Sonnet IV of this cycle.

PART TWO, SONNET XXII

It is our mind that sees the curve of the plane's flight, which actually "makes no mark" upon the sky. It is mind, as the poet asserts in the Ninth Duino Elegy, that "saves" the things:

As if they wanted in our invisible hearts
to be transformed
into—oh, endlessly—into us.

PART TWO, SONNET XXIV

The poet's sense of time here is panoramic. Distant ancestors and future generations take on an almost contemporary immediacy, and the fleeting present moment is enriched by this temporal abundance.

Again, it is our mortality that gives us a hold on life. Our very transience links us with the generations before and the generations to come. In this sense, "all time is ours." We are endlessly offered into life.

PART TWO, SONNET XXVII

To be changed by the passage of time does not mean that anything is really destroyed or fully lost.

PART TWO, SONNET XXIX

This poem has taken on a particular meaning in recent years. Political developments have presented us with an "uncontainable night" and an intensity of pain which these verses help us endure. They help us to keep breathing and to speak out in the darkness.

REFERENCES

MITCHELL, STEPHEN, ed. and trans. *The Selected Poetry of Rainer Maria Rilke.* New York: Random House, 1982.

MITCHELL, STEPHEN, trans. *The Sonnets to Orpheus.* New York: Simon & Schuster, 1985.

The Perfection of Wisdom in Eight Thousand Lines, trans. Edward Conze. Bolinas, CA: Four Seasons Foundation, 1973.

PRATER, DONALD. *A Ringing Glass: The Life of Rainer Maria Rilke.* Oxford: Clarendon Press, and New York: Oxford University Press, 1986.

Rilke's Book of Hours: Love Poems to God, trans. Anita Barrows and Joanna Macy. New York: Riverhead, 1996.

VON SALIS, J. R. [Jean Rodolphe de Salis]. *Rainer Maria Rilke: The Years in Switzerland: A Contribution to the Biography of Rilke's Later Life,* trans. N. K. Cruickshank. Berkeley: University of California Press, 1966.